WITHDRAWN
NDSU

DEATH, DYING and GRIEF

A BIBLIOGRAPHY

by Robert F. Guthmann, Jr.
and Sharon Kay Womack

PIED PUBLICATIONS
LINCOLN, NEBRASKA

BD
444
G87

Copyright © 1978
by Robert F. Guthmann, Jr., and Sharon Kay Womack
All Rights Reserved
Manufactured in the United States of America

Library of Congress Catalog Card Number: 77–82084
International Standard Book Number: 0–918626–01–3

Produced and Distributed by
Pied Publications, 3706 N.W. 51 St., Lincoln, Nebraska 68524

Typesetting by
Quick Keys and Associates, Lincoln, Nebraska

INTRODUCTION

Public and professional interest in the topical areas of dying and bereavement has increased immensely in recent years. All indications point to a continuing interest. The greatest need for information has been generated among the lay public. Whereas the topic of death and dying was considered to be a taboo topic until just a few years ago, it is now an area of discussion. Lay persons are not seeking information on the topic of death to satisfy morbid curiosity. Rather, they are seeking facts which may be used to allay fiction and to prepare for the inevitable, but hopefully distant, future event. Knowledge also is a basis for developing coping skills. Information gained allows the individual to prepare psychologically to meet grieving situations; to cope with both expected and unexpected events; to find alternatives; and to make necessary adjustments in one's lifestyle.

A seemingly desperate need for information on the part of the lay public, the great and diverse variety of resources, an information explosion, and the lack of a concise method of locating information regarding death and its associated topics provided the impetus for assembling this bibliography on death, dying and grief.

Additionally, professionals have been thwarted in their attempts to research topics in their entirety. The difficulty lies with the fact that indexes to professional literature have tended to be narrow in their scope or specific to a topic with little or no cross-referencing.

The authors have attempted to compile a fairly inclusive collection of titles in all areas related to the "death and dying" topics. References include books, journals, printed documents, theses and dissertations, some previously unpublished writings, and a limited number of microfilm and/or microfische entries. The majority of titles were gleaned from the card catalog, Guide to Periodical Literature, Readers Guide, Index Medicus, and trade reference manuals of the University of Nebraska Libraries.

An attempt was made to include materials which were fairly recent. However, there are a few entries which were published more than thirty years ago. The historical researcher's attention is directed to "The Art of Dying Well - The Development of the Ars Moriendi," by Sister Mary Catherine O'Connor, Columbia University Press, New York, 1942, as an excellent source to European works relating to the Middle Ages and early historical accounts. This collection herein contains numerable citations of publications from the 1970's.

In order to assist the reader in locating other sources on the topics reference is made to the following list. No attempt has been made to collate materials found in these bibliographies. No doubt there will be numerous duplications, an expected occurance. However, deference is paid to these authors and their works in an effort to assist others while acknowledging scholarly efforts.

Fulton, Robert. "A Bibliography on Death, Grief and Bereavement (1845-1973)", Third Edition, Center for Death Education and Research, University of Minnesota, 1973.
Berardo, Felix, "Death, Bereavement and Widowhood: A Selective Bibliography", Department of Sociology, Washington State University (mimeographed).
Card catalog, Butler Library, Columbia University, New York.
Card catalog, Kennedy Center for Bioethics, Georgetown University, Washington, D.C.
Card catalog, Library of Congress, Washington, D.C.
Card catalog, Love Memorial Library, University of Nebraska, Lincoln.
Card catalog, National Library of Medicine, National Institute of Health, Bethesda, Maryland.
Cumulative Book Index, H. W. Wilson Co., New York.
Cumulated Index Medicus.
Current Contents: Social and Behavioral Sciences.
General Catalog of Printed Books, British Museum, London.
Kutscher, Austin H., Jr. and Austin H. Kutscher, "A Bibliography of Books on Death, Bereavement, Loss and Grief: 1935-1968," Health Sciences Publishing Corp., New York, 1969; a suppliment.
Kutscher, Martin L. et. al., "A Comprehensive Bibliography of the Thanatology Literature," MSS Information Corporation, New York, 1975.

Readers who are interested in a particular area which includes death as a central theme are encouraged to seek further information in specific references, e.g., art, literature, music, painting, psychology, sociology, education, and so forth.

Hopefully this bibliography will assist interested laymen and professionals alike in their search for information. Included in this listing may be found a wide range of writing styles and efforts, from personal experiences to mood inducing poetry to scholarly tomes. It is the author's hope that this bibliography will prove helpful to those seeking the sources of information on death, dying and grief.

R.F.G.

ARTICLES IN PERIODICALS AND NEWSPAPERS

"A Unit for Independent Study in Death Education". *School Health Review (now Health Education)*, July-August 1973.

Abely, X. and M. Leconte. "Attempt to interpret manic reactions after sorrow". *American Journal of Medical Psychology*, 96:232-240, 1938.

Ablon, Joan. "Bereavement in a Samoan community". *British Journal of Medical Psychology*, 44(4):329-337, 1971.

Abraham, H.S. "The psychology of terminal illness, as portrayed in Solzhenitsyn's, The Cancer Ward". *Archives of Internal Medicine*, 124:758-760, December, 1969.

Abram, H.S. "The psychiatrist, the treatment of chronic renal failure, and the prolongation of life". *American Journal of Psychiatry*, 124:1351-1358, 1968.

Abrams, R.D. and J.E. Finsinger. "Guilt reactions in patients with cancer". *Cancer*, 6:474-482, 1953.

Ackerknecht, E.H. "Death in the history of medicine". *Bulletin of Historical Medicine*, 42:19-23, January-February, 1968.

Adamek, Mary Elaine. "Some observations on death and a family". *Nursing Science*, 3:258-267, August, 1965.

Adelstein, A.M. "Precision in death certification". *Lancet*, 1:682, March 29, 1969.

Adesberger, Lucie. "Aspects of death and dying. The will to live: a journey through the snow". *Journal of the American Medical Women's Association*, 19(6):492-494, June, 1964.

Adler, C.S. "The meaning of death to children". *Arizona Medicine*, 26:266-276, March, 1969.

Aginsky, B.W. "The socio-psychological significance of death among the Pomo Indians". *American Image*, 1:1-11, 1940.

Agnew, Irene. "Will freezing preserve life?". *Science Digest*, 73(6):84-85, December, 1972.

Agree, Rose and Norman Ackerman, "Why children must mourn". *Teacher* (October 1972), pp. 10-16.

Akaishi, S. "Problems concerning death from the viewpoint of legal medicine". *Naika*, 23:861-869, May, 1969.

Alderson, M.R. "Investigation of mortality. Referral to hospital among a representative sample of adults who died". *Proceedings of the Royal Society of Medicine*, 59:719-721, August, 1969.

Aldrich, C. Knight. "The dying patient's grief". *Journal of the American Medical Association*, 184(5):329-331, May 4, 1963.

Alexander, G.H. "An unexplained death coexistent with death wishes". *Psychosomatic Medicine*, 5:188, 1943.

Alexander, I.E. and A.M. Adlerstein. "Affective responses to the concept of death in a population of children and early adolescents". *Journal of Genetic Psychology*, 93:167-177, 1958.

Alexander, I.E., R.S. Colley and A.M. Adlerstein. "Is death a matter of indifference?". *Journal of Psychology*, 43:277-283, 1957.

Alexander, Leo L. "Medical science under dictatorship". *New England Journal of Medicine*, 241(2):39-47, 1949.

Alexander, S. "Flags in the rain". *Life*, 66:4, April 11, 1969.

Alexander, Shana. "They decide who lives, who dies". *Life*, 53(19):102-125, November 9, 1962.

Alfano, Genrose L. "There are no routine patients". *American Journal of Nursing*, 75(10):1804-1807, October, 1975.

"All terminally ill patients can't handle the bad news". *Journal of the American Medical Association*, 229:132, July 8, 1974.

Alsop, Stewart. "The right to die with dignity". *Good Housekeeping*, 179(2):69+, August, 1974.

Altman, Leon L. "West as a symbol of death". *Psychiatric Quarterly*, 28:236-241, 1959.

Alvarez, W.C. "Some aspects of death". *Geriatrics*, 19:465-466, July, 1964.

Anderson, B.G. "Bereavement as a subject of cross-cultural inquiry: an American sample". *Anthropological Quarterly*, 38(4):181-200, 1965.

Anderson, Camilla M. "Aspects of death and dying. Psychology: depression and suicide reassessed". *Journal of the American Medical Women's Association*, 19(6):467-471, June, 1964.

Anderson, Charles. "Aspects of pathological grief and mourning". *International Journal of Psychoanalysis*, 30:38-55, 1949.

Anderson, F. "Who will decide who is to live?". *The New Republic*, 160:9-10, April 19, 1969.

Anger, Diane and Daniel W. "Dialysis ambivalance: a matter of life and death". *American Journal of Nursing*, 76(2):276-277, February, 1976.

Angrist, A.A. "A pathologist's experience with attitudes toward death". *Rhode Island Medical Journal*, 43:693-697, 1960.
Annis, J.W. "The dying patient". *Psychosomatics*, 10:289-292, September-October, 1969.
Ansohn, E. "The physician and the end of life". *Wiener Medizinische Wochenschrift.* 118:1025-1059, November 30, 1968.
Anthony, Sylvia. "A study of the development of death". *British Journal of Educational Psychology*, 9:276-277, 1939.
Aponte, G.E. "The enigma of 'bangungut'". *Annals of Internal Medicine*, 52(6):1258-1263, June, 1960.
Archibald, Herbert D. et. al. "Bereavement in childhood and adult psychiatric disturbances". *Psychosomatic Medicine*, 24:343-351, 1962.
Aradine, Caroline R. "Books for children about death". *Pediatrics*, 57(3) 372-378, March, 1976.
Arehart-Freichel, Joan. "Teaching doctors how to care for the dying". *Science News*, 107:176, March 15, 1975.
Arendt, Hannah. "The concentration camps". *Partisan Review*, 15:747, July, 1948.
Aries, Philippe. "A moment that has lost its meaning". *Prism*, 3(6):27-29, June, 1975.
Aring, C.D. "Intimations of mortality. An appreciation of death and dying". *Annals of Internal Medicine*, 69:137-152, July, 1968.
Aring, Charles D. "A letter from the clinical clerk". *Omega: Journal of Death and Dying*, 1(4):33-34, December, 1966.
Armstrong, R.W. "Standardized class intervals and rate computation in statistical maps of mortality". *Association of American Geographers' Annals*, 59:382-390, June, 1969.
Arnauldsser, Barbara. "Hope". *St. Anthony's Messenger*, 38-42, May, 1976.
Arthur, Bettie and Mary L. Kemme. "Bereavement in childhood". *Journal of Child Psychology and Psychiatry*, 5:37-49, 1964.
Assell, R. "An existential approach to death". *Nursing Forum*, 8:200-211, 1969.
"At home with death". *Newsweek*, 85(1):43-44, January 6, 1975.
"Attitudes towards death". *Intellect*, 103:488-489, May/June, 1975.
Augustin, Demetrio R. "Ceremonies in connection with the dead in Malolos, Bulacan". *Philippine Sociological Review*, 4:32-38, April-June, 1956.

Autton, N. "A study of bereavement, 2 ... to comfort all that mourn". *Nursing Times*, 58:1551-1552, 1962.

Awad, George A. and Elva O. Polznanski. "Psychiatric consultations in a pediatric hospital". *American Journal of Psychiatry*, 132:915-918, September, 1975.

Ayd, Frank J. Jr. "The hopeless case". *Journal of the American Medical Association*, 181(13):1099-1102, 1962.

Azarnoff, Pat. "Medicating the trauma of serious illness and hospitalization in children today". *Children Today*, 3(4):12-17, July-August, 1974.

Bahrmann, E. Et. al. "Problems of determination of death". *Deutsch Gesundh*, 23:2403-2407, December 19, 1968.

Bailey, J. Martin. "Where is the sting of death?". *A.D.*, 4(5):42, May, 1975.

Baker, Betty R. "Grief's slow wisdom". *Power for Living*, 4-6, June 13, 1976.

Baker, J.M. and K.C. Sorensen. "A patient's concern with death". *American Journal of Nursing*, 63:90-92, 1963.

Bakwin, Harry. "Aspects of death and dying. Sociology: suicide in children and adolescents". *Journal of the American Medical Women's Association*, 19(6):489-491, June, 1964.

Baler, Lenin A. and Peggy J. Golde. "Conjugal bereavement: a strategic area of research in preventive psychiatry". *Working Papers in Community Mental Health*, 2, Spring, 1964.

Banks, Sam A. "Dialogue on death: Freudian and Christian views". *Pastoral Psychology*, 14:41-49, 1963.

Bannister, Paul. "Top scientists now convinced there is life after death". *National Enquirer*, 37, June 15, 1976.

Barber, T.X. "Death by suggestion, a critical note". *Psychosomatic Medicine*, 23:153-155, 1961.

Barckley, Virginia. "Families facing cancer". *Cancer News*, Spring/Summer, 1970.

Barckley, Virginia. "What can I say to the cancer patient?". *Nursing Outlook*, 6:316-318, 1958.

Barnacle, Clarke H. "Grief reactions and their treatment". *Diseases of the Nervous System*, 10:173-176, 1940.

Barnard, Charles N. "A good death". *Family Health*, 5:40-42+, April, 1973.

Barnard, Christiaan and Edmund Pellegrino. (Interviews). "The right to die: two views". *Current*, no. 180:46+, February, 1976.

Barnum, Marilyn Clark. "An occupational therapist's observations concerning President Kennedy's assassination; with ramifications for understanding loss". *American Journal of Occupational Therapy*, 20:280-285, December, 1966.

Barrett, G.V. and R.H. Franke. "Psychogenic death". *Science*, 167:304-306, January 16, 1970.

Barry, Herbert. "Orphanhood as a factor in psychoses". *Journal of Abnormal and Social Psychology*, 30:431-438, 1936.

Barry, Herbert. "A study of bereavement; an approach to problems in mental disease". *American Journal of Orthopsychiatry*, 9:355-359, 1939.

Barry, Herbert and W.A. Bousfield. "Incidence of orphanhood among fifteen hundred psychotic patients". *Journal of Genetic Psychology*, 50:198-202, 1937.

Barry, Herbert and Erich Lindemann. "Critical ages for maternal bereavement in psychoneurosis". *Psychosomatic Medicine*, 22:166-181, 1960.

Barry, Herbert, Jr. "Significance of maternal bereavement before the age eight in psychiatric patients". *Archives of Neurological Psychiatry*, 62:630-367, 1949.

Barry, Herbert, Jr., Herbert Barry, III and Erich Lindemann. "Dependency in adult patients following early maternal bereavement". *The Journal of Nervous and Mental Disease*, 140:196-206, 1965.

Bartholomew, A.A. "The personal emergency advisory service". *Mental Hygiene*, 46:382-392, 1962.

Bartholomew, A.A., Margaret F. Kelley, and E.M. Staley. "An analysis of 'night calls' received by a personal emergency telephone service". *Social Service*, 14(5):13, 1963.

Barton, David. "The need for including instruction on death and dying in the medical curriculum". *Journal of Medical Education*, 47:169-175, 1972.

Barton, David. "Teaching psychiatry in the context of dying and death". *American Journal of Psychiatry*, 130:1290-1291, 1973.

Barton, David et. al. "Death and dying: a course for medical students". *Journal of Medical Education*, 47:945-951, 1972.

Bascue, L.O. and G.W. Krieger. "Death as a counseling concern". *Personnel and Guidance journal*, 52:587-592, 1974.

Battle, C.U. "Symposium on behavioral pediatrics. Chronic physical disease. Behavioral aspects". *Pediatric Clinic of North America*, 22:525-531, August, 1975.

Beatty, D. "Shall we talk about death?". *Pastoral Psychology*, 6:11-14, 1955.

Beauner, Robert. "Death and social structure". *Psychiatry*, 29:378-394, 1966.

Beck, Aaron T., Brij B. Sethi and R.W. Tuthill. "Childhood bereavement and adult depression". *Archives of General Psychiatry*, 9:295-302, 1963.

Becker, D. and F. Margolin. "How surviving parents handled their young children's adaptations to the crisis of loss". *American Journal of Orthopsychiatry*, 37:753-757, 1967.

Becker, Ernst. "Toward a comprehensive theory of depression; a cross disciplinary appraisal of objects, games and meaning". *Journal of Nervous and Mental Disorders*, 135:26-35, 1962.

Becker, H. "The sorrow of bereavement". *Journal of Abnormal and Social Psychology*, 27:391-410, 1933.

Becker, Howard and David K. Bruner. "Attitudes toward death and the dead and some possible causes of ghost fear". *Mental Hygiene*, 15:828-837, 1931.

Beecher, H.K. "After the 'definition of irreversible coma'". *New England Journal of Medicine*, 281:1070-1071, November 6, 1969.

Beecher, Henry K. "Nonspecific forces surrounding disease and the treatment of disease". *Journal of the American Medical Association*, 179(6):437-440, 1962.

Behm, H. "Recent mortality trends in Chile". *Vital Health Statistics*, 3:1-34, 1964.

Beidelman, T.O. "Three tales of the living and the dead: the ideology of Kaguru ancestral propitiation". *Journal of the Royal Anthropological Institute of Great Britain and Ireland*, 94(1):109-137, July-December, 1964.

Beigler, Jerome S. "Anxiety as an aid in the prognostication in impending death". *Archives of Neurological Psychiatry*, 77:171-177, 1957.

Beigner, Jerome S. "Anxiety as an aid in the prognostication of impending death". *American Medical Association Archives of Neurology and Psychiatry*, 77:171-177, 1957.

Bell, David. "The baby who refused to die". *Good Housekeeping*, 180(5):98+, May, 1975.

Bell, Joseph N. "Today is the important day - the only important day". *Good Housekeeping*, 180(4):83+, April, 1975.

Benda, Dr. Clemens E. "Bereavement and grief work". *Journal of Pastoral Care*, 16:1-13, 1962.

Bendiksen, R. and R. Fulton. "Death and the child: an anterospective test of the childhood bereavement and later behavior disorder hypothesis". *Omega: Journal of Death and Dying*, 6(1):45-59, 1975.

Benezra, E.E. "Duality of human nature". *American Journal of Psychiatry*, 125:1456-1457, April, 1969.

Berardo, Felix M. "Survivorship and social isolation: the case of the aged widowers". *The Family Coordinator*, 19(1):11-25, January, 1970.

Berg, C.D. "Cognizance of the death taboo in counseling children". *School Counselor*, 21:28-33, 1973.

Berg, David W. and George G. Daugherty. "Teaching about death". *Today's Education*, 62(3):46-47, March, 1973.

Berg, S. "The value of the determination of time of death (survival time)". *Beitraege zur Gerichtlichen Medizin*, 25:61-65, 1969.

Berger, Adolph R. "Ethical implications of professional competency". *The Journal of the American Medical Association*, 200:1008, June 12, 1967.

Berger, P.F. and C.A. Berger. "Death on demand. Discussions". *Commweal*, 103:99, February 13, 1976; 103:255, April 7, 1976.

Berger, Patrick F. and Carol A. "Death on demand". *Commonweal*, 102(19):585-589, December 5, 1975.

Bergler, Edmund. "Psychopathology and duration of mourning in neurotics". *Journal of Clinical Psychopathology*, 3:478-482, 1948.

Bergman, A.B. "Crib deaths exact needless toll of grief in infants' families". *Hospital Topics*, 47:69-73, February, 1969.

Berman, Eric. "Death terror; observations of interaction patterns in an American family". *Omega: Journal of Death and Dying*, 4:275-291, 1973.

Bernstein, Ellen. "Suicide prevention. Finding help when it is needed most". *Today's Health*, 54(2):48-49, February, 1976.

Bettelheim, B. "Dialogue with mother: when a child asks: 'Am I going to die?'". *Ladies' Home Journal*, 83:24+, November, 1966.

Beverley, E. Virginia. "Understanding and helping dying patients and their families". *Geriatrics*, 31(3):117+, March, 1976.

Billow, Carol and Barbara Johnson. "Help for the child in crisis". *School Health Review*, 4(1):22-23, 1973.

Binder, Barton J. "Sibling death in childhood". *Child Psychiatry and Human Development*, 2(4):169, Summer, 1972.

Binger, C.M. et al. "Childhood leukemia; emotional impact on patient and family". *New England Journal of Medicine*, 280:414-418, 1969.

Biran, S. "Attempt at the psychological analysis of the fear of death". *Confinia Psychiatrica*, 11:154-176, 1968.

Birk, Alma. "The bereaved child". *Mental Health*, 25(4):9-11, 1966.

Birtchnell, John. "The possible consequences of early parent death". *British Journal of Medical Psychology*, 42:1-12, 1969.

Black, Peter McL. "Focusing on some of the ethical problems associated with death and dying". *Geriatrics*, 31(1):138-141, January, 1976.

Blanchely, P.H., William Disher and Gregory Rodenver. "Suicide by physicians". *Bulletin of Suicidology*, 1-18, 1967.

Blank, H. "Crisis consultation". *International Journal of Social Psyciatry*, 21:179-189, Autumn, 1975.

Blank, Joseph P. "Two seconds to live". *Reader's Digest*, 109(651):81-84, July, 1976.

Blaske, Lee. "A sociologist looks at death and dying". *Linacre Quarterly*, 42(4):256-261, November, 1975.

Blauner, Robert. "Death and social structure". *Psychiatry*, 29(4):378-394, 1966.

Blazer, John A. "The relationship between meaning in life and fear of death". *Psychology*, 10:33-34, 1973.

Bliss, V. Jane. "Sharing another's death". *Nursing*, 6(3):52-56, 1976.

Bloom, Sholom. "On teaching an undergraduate course on death and dying". *Omega: Journal of Death and Dying*, 6:223-225, 1975.

Bluestone, Harvey and Carl L. McGhee. "Reaction to extreme stress; death by execution". *American Journal of Psychiatry*, 119(5):393-396, 1962.

Blum, G.S. and S. Rosenzweig. "The incidence of sibling and parental deaths in the anamenesis of female schizophrenics". *Journal of General Psychology*, 31:3-13, 1944.

Bock, E. Wilber. "Aging and suicide: the significance of marital, kinship and alternative relations". *The Family Coordinator*, 21(1):71-79, January, 1972.

Bock, Wilbur and Irving Webber. "Suicide among the elderly: isolating widowhood and mitigating alternatives". *Journal of Marriage and the Family*, 34(1):24-30, February, 1972.

Borel, C.M. "Defining death". *General Practitioner*, 39:171-178, January, 1969.

Borkenau, Franz. "The concept of death". *The Twentieth Century*, 157:313-329, 1955.

Bose, A.B. and M.L.A. Sen. "Some characteristics of the widows in rural society". *Man in India*, 46(3):226-232, 1966.

Boskin, Warren. "A case for crisis education". *School Health Review*, 2(4):25-27, 1971.

Bourjaily, Monte, Jr. "A pretty good teacher, for a cat". *Reader's Digest*, 98:82-36, March, 1971.

Bowlby, John. "Childhood mourning and its implications for psychiatry". *American Journal of Psychiatry*, 118:481-498, 1961.

Bowlby, John. "Grief and mourning in infancy and early childhood". *The Psychoanalytic Association*, 11:500-541, 1960.

Bowlby, John. "The nature of the child's tie to his mother". *The International Journal of Psychoanalysis*, 39:1-23, 1958.

Bowlby, John. "Pathological mourning and childhood mourning". *Journal of the American Psychoanalytic Association*, 11:500-541, 1963.

Bowlby, John. "Process of mourning". *International Journal of Psychoanalysis*, 42:317-340, 1961.

Bowlby, John. "Separation anxiety". *International Journal of Psychoanalysis*, 41:89-113, 1960.

Bowlby, John. "Some pathological processes engendered by early mother-child separation". *British Journal of Psychiatry*, 99:265-272, 1953.

Branscomb, Allan and Elbert Branscomb. "Sharing: a death research information exchange". *Omega: Journal of Death and Dying*, 4:243-249, 1973.

Branson, Roy. "Is acceptance a denial of death? Another look at Kubler-Ross". *The Christian Century*, 92:464-468, May 7, 1975.

Brantner, John P. "I speak for the funeral". *The Director*, the official publication of The National Funeral Directors Association, 11, May, 1972.

Brauer, Paul H. "Should the patient be told the truth?". *Nursing Outlook*, 8(12):672, December, 1960.

"Breaking funeral directors' monopoly". *Christian Century*, 81:423, April 1, 1964.

Breed, J.E. "New questions in medical morality". *Illinois Medical Journal*, 135:504+, April, 1969.

Brett, L. "The revised funeral rites". *The Living Light*, 7:71-83, Spring, 1970.

Breuer, Judith. "Sharing a tragedy". *American Journal of Nursing*, 76(5):758-759, May, 1976.

Brewster, Henry H. "Grief: a disrupted human relationship". *Human Organization*, 9:19-22, 1950.

Brewster, Henry H. "Separation reaction in psychosomatic disease and neurosis". *Psychosomatic Medicine*, 14:154-160, 1952.

Brill, A.A. "Thoughts on life and death or Vidonian All Souls' Eve". *Psychiatric Quarterly*, 21:199-211, 1947.

Brockopp, Gene W. and Allen Yasser. "Training the volunteer telephone therapist". *Crisis Intervention*, 2:65-77, 1970.

Brodsky, Bernard. "Liebstod fantasies in a patient faced with a fatal illness". *International Journal of Psychoanalysis*, 40(1):13-16, January-February, 1959.

Brodsky, Bernard. "The self-representation, anality and the fear of dying". *Journal of the American Psychoanalytic Association*, 7(1):95-108, January, 1959.

Brody, Matthew. "Compassion for life and death". *Medical Opinion and Review*, 3(1):108-113, January, 1967.

Bromberg, W. and P. Schilder. "The attitude of psychoneurotics towards death". *Psychoanalytic Review*, 23(1):1-25, 1955.

Bromberg, Walter and Paul Schilder. "Death and dying". *Psychoanalytic Review*, 20:133-185, 1933.

Brook, J. "Ways of death: concerning three books on funeral industry". *Consumer Reports*, 29:40-43, January, 1964.

Brown, M.D. et. al. "The preservation of life". *Journal of the American Medical Association*, 211:76-82, January 5, 1970.

Brown, Felix. "Depression and childhood bereavement". *Journal of Mental Science*, 107:754-777, 1961.

Brown, Paula. "Chimbu death payments". *Journal of the Royal Anthropological Institute of Great Britain and Ireland*, 91(1):77-96, January-June, 1961.

Bruce, Sylvia J. "Reactions of nurses and mothers to still births". *Nursing Outlook*, 10:88-91, February, 1962.

Bruhn, John G. et. al. "Patients' reactions to death in a coronary care unit". *Journal of Psychosomatic Research*, 14:65-70, 1970.

Boyle, Ivy R. et. al. "Emotional adjustment of adolescents and young adults with cystic fibrosis". *Journal of Pediatrics*, 88:318-326, February, 1976.

Buchanan, William. "John Baker's last race". *Reader's Digest*, 107(640):56-61, August, 1975.

Bulger, Roger. "The dying patient and his doctor". *Harvard Medical Alumni Bulletin*, 34(3):23-25, 53-57, 1960.

Bulger, Roger J. "Doctors and dying". *Archives of Internal Medicine*, 112:327-332, September, 1963.

Bullough, Vern L. "The banal and costly funeral". *The Humanist*, 4:312-318, 1960.

Burnham, Donald _. "Separation anxiety - a factor in the object relations of schizophrenic patients". *Archives of General Psychiatry*, 13:346-358, October, 1965.

Burton, Arthur. "Death as a countertransference". *Psychoanalysis and the Psychoanalytic Review*, 49:3-20, 1962.

Buxbaum, Robert E. "Grief begins not with death, but with knowing it is near". *Texas Medicine*, 62:44-45, October, 1966.

Bynum, Jack. "Social status and rites of passage: the social context of death". *Omega: Journal of Death and Dying*, 4:323-332, 1973.

Cain, A.C. and J. Fast. "Children's disturbed reactions to parent suicide". *American Journal of Orthopsychiatry*, 36:873-880, October, 1966.

Cain, Albert C. "The presuperego 'turning inward' of agression". *The Psychoanalytic Quarterly*, 30:171-208, April, 1961.

Cain, Albert C. et al. "Children's disturbed reactions to their mother's miscarriage". *Psychosomatic Medicine*, 24:58-66, 1964.

Cain, Albert C. and Barbara S. Cain. "On replacing a child", digest of paper presented at meeting of American Orthopsychiatric Association. *American Journal of Orthopsychiatry*, 32:297-298, 1962.

Cain, Albert C., Irene Fast, and Mary Erickson. "Children's reactions to the death of a sibling". *American Journal of Orthopsychiatry*, 32:297-298, 1962.

Caldwell, Diane and Brian L. Mishara. "Research on attitudes of medical doctors toward the dying patient: a methodological problem". *Omega: Journal of Death and Dying*, 3(4):341-346, 1972.

Calloway, N.O. "Patterns of senile death". *Journal of the American Geriatric Society*, 14:156-166, February, 1966.

Cameron, P. "The imminency of death". *Journal of Consulting Clinical Psychology*, 32:479-481, August, 1968.

Cameron, P., Stewart, L., and Biber, H. "Consciousness of death across the life-span". *Journal of Gerontology*, 28(1):92-95, 1973.

Campbell, Colin. "How nurses view the face of death". *Psychology Today*, 9(7):123+, December, 1975.

Campbell, H. "Changes in mortality trends: England Wales". *Vital Health Statistics*, 3:1-49, November, 1965.

Cannon, Walter B. "'Voodoo' death". *American Anthropologist*, 4:169-181, 1942.

Capon, R.F. "Secular and the sacred". *America*, 116:307-312, March 4, 1967.

Cappon, Daniel. "Attitudes of and towards the dying". *Canadian Medical Association Journal*, 87:693-700, 1962.

Cappon, Daniel. "Attitudes on death". *Omega: Journal of Death and Dying*, 1:103-108, 1970.

Cappon, Daniel. "The dying". *Psychiatric Quarterly*, 33:466-489, 1959.

Caprio, F.S. "Ethnological attitudes toward death: a psychoanalytic evaluation". *Journal of Clinical and Experimental Psychopathology*, 7:737-752, 1946.

Caprio, F.S. "A psycho-social study of primitive conception of death". *Journal of Criminal Psychopathology*, 5:303-317, 1943.

Caprio, F.S. "A study of psychological reactions during prepubescence to the idea of death". *Psychiatric Quarterly*, 24:495-505, 1950.

Capron, Alexander Morgan and Leon R. Kass. "A statutory definition of the standards for determining human death: an appraisal and a proposal". *University of Pennsylvania Law Review*, 121(1):87-118, November, 1972.

Carey, Raymond G. "Emotional adjustment in terminal patients: a quantitative approach". *Journal of Counseling Psychology*, 21(5):433-439, 1974.

Carlinsky, Don. "Teenage suicide". *Sr. Scholastic*, 104:13-15, February 7, 1974.

Carmichael, B. "The death wish in daily life". *Psychoanalytic Review*, 30:59-66, 1943.

Carnell, E.J. "Fear of death". *Christian Century*, 80:136-137, 1963.

Carnes, Paul N. "The fact of death". *The Register-Leader of the Unitarian Universalist Association*, 148:10-11, October, 1966.

Carpenter, Edmund S. "Eternal life and self-definition among the Aivilik Eskimos". *American Journal of Psychiatry*, 110:840-843, 1954.

Carpenter, James O. and Charles M. Wylie. "On aging, dying and denying: delivering care to older dying patients". *Public Health Reports*, 89(5):403-407, 1974.

Carstairs, G.M. "Attitudes to death and suicide in an Indian cultural setting". *International Journal of Social Psychiatry*, 1:33-41, 1955.

Carr, J.L. "The coroner and the common law, III. Death and its medical imputations". *California Medicine*, 93:32-34, 1960.

Casberg, Melvin A. "The patient as a 'whole man'". *Journal of the American Medical Association*, 201(1):72, July 3, 1967.

Casberg, Melvin A. "Toward human values in medical practice". *Medical Opinion and Review*, 3(5):22-25, 1967.

Cash, Larry M. and Earl W. Kooker. "Attitudes toward death of NP patients who have attempted suicide". *Psychological Reports*, 26:879-882, 1970.

Cassell, E.J. "Death and the physician". *Commentary*, 47:73-74, June, 1969.

Cassell, Eric J. "Permission to die". *Bioscience*, 23(8):475-478, August, 1973.

Cavanagh, John. "Bene mori; the right of the patient to die with dignity". *Linacre Quarterly*, 42(3):157-167, August, 1975.

Chadwick, Mary. "Notes upon fear of death". *International Journal of Psychoanalysis*, 10:321-334, 1929.

Chaloner, Len. "How to answer the questions children ask about death". *Parent's Magazine*, 37:48+, November, 1962.

Chambers, J. et. al. "The mortalogram - an epidemiological device employed in a quinquennial study of mortality in Omaha, Douglas County, 1880-1960". *Nebraska Medical Journal*, 49:308-313, 1964.

Chandler, Kenneth A. "Three processes of dying and their behavioral effects". *Journal of Consulting Psychology*, 29:296-301, 1965.

Chandra, R.K. "A child dies". *Indian Journal of Pediatrics*, 35:363-364, July, 1968.

Chaney, Patricia. "Surviving". *Nursing*, 6(4):41-50, April, 1976.

"Changing way of death". *Time*, 93:60, April 11, 1969.

Chasin, B. "Neglected variables in the study of death attitudes". *Sociological Quarterly*, 12:107-113, 1971.

Chernus, Jack. "Let them die with dignity". *Riss*, 7(6):73-86, 1964.

"Children view death in many ways". *Science Digest*, 73:88-89, May, 1973.

Chodoff, Paul et. al. "Stress, defenses and coping behavior: observations in parents of children with malignant disease". *American Journal of Psychiatry*, 120:743-749, 1964.

Chodorff, P. "A psychiatric approach to the dying patient". *Cancer*, 10:29-32, 1960.

Christ, A.E. "Attitudes toward death among a group of acute geriatric psychiatric patients". *Journal of Gerontology*, 16:56-59, 1961.

Christenson, L. "The physician's role in terminal illness and death". *Minnesota Medicine*, 46-:881-883, 1963.

"Christian service for the dead". *America*, 129:183-184, February 15, 1969.

Christopherson, Lois K. "Cardiac transplant: preparation for dying or for living." *Health and Social Work*, 1(1):58-72, 1975.

Christy, G. "Dad's last good-bye". *Good Housekeeping*, 168:89+, April, 1969.

Church, Frank. "I was told I had six months to live". *Good Housekeeping*, 182(1):26+, 1976.

Ciocco, A. "On the mortality in husbands and wives". *Human Biology*, 12:508-531, 1940.

Ciocco, A. et. al. "Four years mortality experience of a segment of the United States working population". *American Journal of Public Health*, 5:587-595, 1965.

Clark, Margie B. "A therapeutic approach to treating a grieving 2½ year old". *Journal of the American Academy of Child Psychiatry*, 11:705-711, 1972.

Clark, Matt. "Clues to crib death". *Newsweek*, 87(1):53, January 5, 1976.

Clark, Matt and Susan Agrest. "A right to die". *Newsweek*, 86(18):58-60+, November 3, 1975.

Clarke, K.S. "Calculated risk of sports fatalities". *Journal of American Medical Association*, 197:894-896, September, 1966.

Clayton, P. et. al. "A study of normal bereavement". *American Journal of Psychiatry*, 125:168-178, August, 1968.

Cleaveland, F.P. "The dance of death". *Journal of the American Medical Association*, 176:142-143, 1961.

Cleaveland, F.P. "Masquerades: homicide, suicide, accident or natural death". *Journal of Indiana Medical Association*, 53:2181-2184, 1960.

Cleaver, J.H. "Preventing suicide". *Medical Herald*, (St. Joseph), 49:47-95, 1967.

Cleghom, Sarah N. "Changing thoughts of death". *Atlantic Monthly*, 132:808, 1923.

Clouse, G.D. "Introductions to widowhood. The role of the family physician". *Ohio Medical Journal*, 62:1281-1284, December, 1966.

Cobb, Beatrix. "Psychological impact of long illness and death of a child on the family circle". *Journal of Pediatrics*, 39:746-751, 1956.

Cochrane, A.L. "Elie Metschnikoff and his theory of an 'instinct de la mort'". *International Journal of Psychoanalysis*, 15:265-270, 1934.

Cochrane, A.L. "A little widow is a dangerous thing". *International Journal of Psychoanalysis*, 17:494, 1936.

Coffey, Pat. "When is killing the unborn a homicidal action?". *Linacre Quarterly*, 43(2):85-92, May, 1976.

Cohen, B.H. "Family patterns of mortality and life span". *Quarterly Review of Biology*, 39:130-181, 1964.

Cohen, M. and L.M. Lipton. "Spontaneous remission of schizophrenic psychoses following maternal death". *Psychiatric Quarterly*, 24:716-725, 1950.

Cohen, Sidney. "LSD and the anguish of dying". *Harper's Magazine*, 231(1384):69-78, September, 1965.

Collett, Lora J. and David Lester. "The fear of death and the fear of dying". *Journal of Psychology*, 72(2):179-181, 1969.

Collette, Clara L. "Death with dignity: unsolicited responses to a gubernatorial statement". *The Gerontologist*, 13(3):327-331, Autumn, 1973.

Comfort, Alex. "On gerontophobia". *Medical Opinion and Review*, 3(9):30-37, 1967.

Conley, J.C. "Editorial rights of the dying patient". *Archives of Otolaryngology*, 90:405, October, 1969.

Connell, E.H. "The significance of the idea of death in the neurotic mind". *British Journal of Medical Psychology*, 4:115-124, 1924.

Connery, S.J. "The Quinlan case". *Linacre Quarterly*, 43(1):25-29, 1976.

Coolidge, J.C. "Unexpected death in a patient who wished to die". *Journal of the American Psycoanalytic Association*, 17:413-420, April, 1969.

Cooper, Philip. "The fabric we weave". *Medical Opinion and Review*, 3(1):36, January, 1967.

"Coping with death in the family". *Business Week*, No. 2426:93+, April 5, 1976.

Corey, Lawrence G. "An analogue of resistance to death awareness". *Journal of Gerontology*, 16:59-60, 1961.

Corrigan, J. "Future revisions of the anointing of the sick". *Homiletic and Pastoral Review*, 68:600-602, April, 1968.

Cort, D. "Another visit to the undertaker". *Nation*, 200:420-421, April 19, 1965.

Costa, Paul T. and R. Kastenbaum. "Some aspects of memories and ambitions in centenarians". *Journal of Genetic Psychology*, 110:3-16, 1967.

Covill, F.J. "Bereavement--a public health challenge". *Canadian Journal of Public Health*, 59:169-170, April, 1968.

Cox, Peter and John R. Ford. "The mortality of widows shortly after widowhood". *The Lancet*, 1:163-164, 1964.

Crafoord, C.C. "Cerebral death and the transplantation era". *Diseases of the Chest*, 55:141-145, February, 1969.

Craig, Delores Bonse. "The good days of life - and the last". *RN*, 39(4):51-56, April, 1976.

Cramond, W.A. "Psychotherapy of the dying patient". *British Medical Journal*, 3(5719):389-393, August, 1970.

Crase, Dixie R. and Darrell Crase. "Death and the young child". *Clinical Pediatrics*, 14(8):747-750, August, 1975.

Crase, Dixie R. and Darrell Crase. "Live issues surrounding death education". *The Journal of School Health*, 44(2):70-73, 1974.

Craven, Joan and Florence S. Wald. "Hospice care for the dying patients". *American Journal of Nursing*, 75(10):1816-1822, October, 1975.

Craytor, Josephine K. "Talking with persons who have cancer". *American Journal of Nursing*, 69(4):744+, April, 1969.

Creegan, R.F. "A symbolic action during bereavement". *Journal of Abnormal and Social Psychology*, 37:403-405, 1942.

Crook, Thomas and Allen Raskin. "Association of childhood parental loss with attempted suicide and depression". *Journal of Consulting and Clinical Psychology*, 43(2):277, April, 1975.

Curran, William J. "An enigma wrapped in swaddling clothes: Congress and 'crib death'". *New England Journal of Medicine*, 287(5):235-237, August 3, 1972.

Custer, H.R. "Nursing care of the dying". *Hospital Programs*, 42:68, 1961.

Cutler, Ann and R.C.W. Ettinger. "New hope for the dead". *Esquire*, 63:63+, May, 1965.

Cutler, Donald R. "Death and responsibility: a minister's view". *Psychiatric Opinion*, 3(4):8-12, 1966.

Davis, Christopher. "Death in sun city". *Esquire*, 133-137: October, 1966.

Davis, F. "Uncertainty in medical prognosis". *American Journal of Sociology*, 66:41-47, July, 1960.

Davis, J.A. "The attitude of parents to the approaching death of their child". *Developmental Medicine and Child Neurology*, 6:286-288, 1964.

Davis, K. "The widow and the social structure". *American Sociological Review*, 5:635-647, August, 1940.

Day, Ingeborg. "Mark, a dairy of a son's dying". *Ms. Magazine*, 4:54-56+, February, 1976.
De, A.K. et. al. "Abridged life tables for rural India". *Milbank Memorial Fund Quarterly*, 42:96-108, 1964.
"Death... a concept to reconsider". *Journal of the Florida Medical Association*, 56:799, October, 1969.
"Death: A part of life". *Current Health*, 3(7):_, March 1977.
"Death and transplantation". *Hospitals*, 43:47, November 1, 1969.
"Death companionship". *Time*, 105(7):68, February 17, 1975.
"Death in a cancer ward". *Time*, 93:62+, June 20, 1969.
"Death in America". *Scientific American*, 216:56, February, 1967.
"Death in childhood". *Canadian Medical Association Journal*, 98:967-969, May 18, 1968.
"Death: the way of life". *Harvest Years*, 9:19-34, April, 1969.
"Death without dignity". *Time*, 104(1):58-59, July 1, 1974.
"Decline in infant and child mortality". *World Health Organization Chronicle*, 19:112-115, 1965.
De Dellarossa, G.S. "The concept of death in your self-development". *Revista de Psicoanalysis*, 22:26-44, 1965.
Deegan, Mary Jo. "The symbolic passage from the living to the dead for the visibly injured". *International Journal of Symbology*, 6(3):1-13, November, 1975.
"Defining death". *Time*, 105(10):76, March 10, 1975.
"Definition of death". *Science Digest*, 65:77, March, 1969.
DeJarast, S.G. "Mourning in relation to learning". *Revista de Psicoanalysis*, 15:31-35, 1958.
Deutsch, Felix. "Euthanasia: a clinical study". *The Psychoanalytic Quarterly*, 5:347-368, 1936.
Deutsch, Helene. "Absence of grief". *Psychoanalytic Quarterly*, 6:12-22, 1937.
Devereux, George. "Funeral suicide and the Mohave social structure: primitive Psychiatry". *Bulletin of the History of Medicine*, 11:522-542, 1942.
Devereux, George. "Social structure and the economy of affective bonds". *Psychoanalytic Review*, 29:303-314, 1942.
DeVos, George and Hiroshi Wagatsume. "Psycho-cultural significance of concern over death and illness among rural Japanese". *International Journal of Social Psyciatry*, 5:5-19, 1959.

Dewart, L. "The fact of death". *Commonweal*, 91:206-208, November 14, 1969.

"Dialogue on death: physician and patient". *Geriatric Focus*, 5:1+, February, 1966.

Dickstein, Louis S. and Sidney J. Blatt. "Death concern, futurity and anticipation". *Journal of Consulting Psychology*, 30(1):11-17, 1966.

Diggory, James C. and Doreen Z. Rothman. "Values destroyed by death". *Journal of Abnormal and Social Psychology*, 63:205-210, 1961.

Dizmang, Larry. "Suicide among the Cheyenne Indians". *Bulletin of Suicidology*, :8-11, July, 1967.

Dobzhansky, Theodosius. "An essay on religion, death and evolutonary adaptation". *Zygon - Journal of Religion and Science*, 1(4):317-331, December, 1966.

Dodge, Joan S. "How much should the patient be told - and by whom?". *Hospitals*, 37:66-70, December 16, 1963.

Dorf, Ilene. "Quinlan case leaves physicians with life-death decisions". *Hospitals*, 50(1):83-85, January 1, 1976.

Dorn, H.F. et. al. "Uses and significance of multiple cause tabulations for mortality statistics". *American Journal of Public Health*, 54:400-406, 1964.

Dorpat, T.L. "Loss of control over suicidal impulses". *Bulletin of Suicidology*, 26-30, 1967.

Draughon, Margaret. "Step-mother's model of identification in relation to mourning in the child". *Psychological Reports*, 36(1):183-189, 1975.

Dresner, Sanuel H. "The scandal of the Jewish funeral". *The Torch*, 6-22, Spring, 1963.

Driver, M.V. "EEG and the declaration of death". *Electroencephalography and Clinical Neurophysiology*, 27:332, September, 1969.

Dukeminier, J., Jr. "Supplying organs for transplantation". *Michigan Law Review*, 68:811-866, 1970.

Dunn, J.A. "What happens to you after you die?". *U.S. Catholic*, 37:6-12, November, 1972.

Dunn, P.M. et. al. "Infant and child mortality in South Warwickshire, 1962-1963". *Archives of Disease in Childhood*, 39:492-495, 1964.

Durlak, Joseph. "Relationship between individual attitudes toward life and death". *Journal of Consulting and Clinical Psychology*, 38:463, 1972.

Drummond, Eleanor and Jeanne Blumberg. "Death and the curriculum". *Journal of Nursing Education*, 1:21-28, May-June, 1962.

Dyck, A.J. "Perplexities for the would be liberal in abortion". *Journal of Reproductive Medicine*, 8(6):351-354, June, 1972.

Dyck, A.J. "Questions for the global conscience". *Psychology Today*, 2(4):38-42, 1965.

"A dying child's sense of isolation". *Science News*, 107:23, January 11, 1975.

"Dying - out of darkness". *Time*, 94(15):60, October 10, 1969.

Dynes, J.B. "Sudden death". *Diseases of the Nervous System*, 30:24-28, January, 1969.

Earle, A.M. and B.V. Earle. "Early maternal deprivation and later psychiatric illness". *American Journal of Orthopsychiatry*, 31:181-186, 1961.

Earley, Harold W.J. "A funeral is for the living". *The Lutheran*, 15-17, January 4, 1967.

Easson, Eric C. "Cancer and the problem of pessimism". *CA, A Cancer Journal for Clinicians*, 17(1):7-14, January-February, 1967.

Eaton, Joseph W. "The art of aging and dying". *The Gerontologist*, 14(2):94-100, 1964.

Edelson, Stuart R. and Porter H. Warren. "Catatonic schizophrenia as a mourning process". *Diseases of the Nervous System*, 24:2-8, 1963.

"Education for Death". *Journal of Health, Physical Education and Recreation*, 40(7): 46-51, September, 1969.

"Effects of bereavement". *Canadian Medical Association Journal*, 90:668, 1964.

"Effects of experiences with loss and death among preschool children". *Children Today*, 2-7, November-December, 1975.

Eidelman, J.R. "Prevention of suicide". *Journal of Missouri Medical Association*, 48:441-446, 1951.

Eisenberg, P.B. "Rest in peace, ruthless Roger". *American Journal of Nursing*, 70:132, January, 1970.

Eisendrath, R.M. "The role of grief and fear in the death of kidney transplant patients". *Association of Operating Room Nurses Journal*, 11:71+, January, 1970.

Eisenthal, S. "Death ideation in suicidal patients". *Journal of Abnormal Psychology*, 73:162-167, April, 1968.

Ekblom, B. "On mortality in recent widows and widowers". *Svenska Lakartidningen*, 61:3343-3350, 1964.

Ekblom, B. "The significance of social psychological factors for the death risk, especially in aged persons". *Nordisk Psykiatrisk Tidsskrift*, 18:272-281, 1964.

Eliot, T. "The bereaved family". *Annals of the American Academy of Political and Social Science*, 160:184-190, March, 1932.

Eliot, Thomas D. "The adjustive behavior of bereaved families: a new field for research". *Social Forces*, 8:543-549, 1930.

Eliot, Thomas D. "Attitudes toward euthanasia". *Research Studies of the State College of Washington*, 14:131-134, 1947.

Eliot, Thomas D. "Bereavement as a field of social research". *Bulletin of the Society for Social Research*, 17:4, 1938.

Eliot, Thomas D. "Bereavement as a problem for family research and technique". *The Family*, 11:114-115, 1930.

Eliot, Thomas D. "Of the shadow of death". *Annals of the American Academy of Political and Social Science*, 229:87-99, 1943.

Eliot, Thomas D. "A step toward the social psychology of bereavement". *Journal of Abnormal and Social Psychology*, 27:380-390, 1933.

Eliot, Thomas D. "War bereavements and their recovery". *Marriage and Family Living*, 8:1-6, 1946.

Elkinton, J.R. "The Literature of ethical problems in medicine - Part 3". *Annals of Internal Medicine*, 73:863-870, 1970.

Elkinton, J.R. "Moral problems in the use of borrowed organs, artificial and transplanted". *Annals of Internal Medicine*, 69:309-313, 1964.

Elkinton, J. Russel. "The experimental use of human beings". *Annals of Internal Medicine*, 65:371-373, August, 1966.

Ellis, R.S. "The attitude toward death and the types of belief in immortality". *Journal of Religious Psychology*, 7:466, 1915.

"Emotions and sudden death". *Science News*, 109(13):199, March 27, 1976.

Engel, George L. "Grief and grieving". *American Journal of Nursing*, 64:93-98, September, 1964.

Engel, George L. "Sudden and rapid death during psychological stress: folklore or folk wisdom?". *Current Medical Dialog*, 305, March, 1972. Also available in *Annals of Internal Medicine*, 74:771, 1971.

Engel, George L. "Is grief a disease?". *Psychosomatic Medicine*, 23:18-22, 1961.

Epstein, L.C. and L. Lasagna. "Obtaining informed consent". *Archives of Internal Medicine*, 123:682, 1969.

Etzioni, Amitai. "Life, dying, death, ethics and open decision". *Science News*, 106(7):109-111, August 17, 1964.

"Euthanasia and the law". *Newsweek*, 83:45, January 28, 1974.

"Euthanasia at 80? Proposal by British Public Health Official". *Newsweek*, 73:77, May 12, 1969.

Evans, P.R. "The management of fatal illness in childhood". *Proceedings of the Royal Society of Medicine*, 62:549-550, June, 1969.

Evelson, E. and R. Grinberg. "The child's concept of death". *Revista de Psicoanalyisis*, 19:344-350, 1962.

Fairbairn, W.R.D. "The effect of the king's death upon patients under analysis". *International Journal of Psychoanalysis*, 17:278-284, 1936.

Fairbanks, Rollin J. "Ministering to the dying". *Journal of Pastoral Care*, 2:6-14, 1948.

Farberow, Norman L. "Suicide prevention around the clock". *American Journal of Orthopsychiatry*, 36(3):551-558, 1966.

Farberow, Norman L. and Sharon Y, Moriwaki. "Self-destructive crises in the older person". *The Gerontologist*, 15(4):333-337, August, 1975.

"Farewell to Eisenhower". *U.S. News and World Report*, 66:68, April 14, 1969.

Farker, Thomas. "Reflections of an angry pastor". *Linacre Quarterly*, 42(4):250-254, November, 1975.

Fast, Irene and Albert C. Cain. "Fears of death in bereaved children and adults". *American Journal of Orthopsychiatry*, 34:278-279, 1964.

Faunce, William A. and Robert Fulton. "The sociology of death: a neglected area of research". *Social Forces*, 36:305-309, March, 1958.

Federn, Paul. "The reality of the death instinct". *Psychoanalytic Review*, 19:129-150, 1932.
Feibleman, Peter. "The haunted city". *Holiday*, 29:88-89, June, 1961.
Feifel, Herman. "Attitudes of mentally ill patients toward death". *Journal of Nervous and Mental Disease*, 122:375-380, 1955.
Feifel, Herman. "Attitudes toward death: a psychological perspective". *Journal of Consulting and Clinical Psychology*, 33:292-295, 1969.
Feifel, Herman. "Discussion of a symposium on attitudes toward death in older persons". *Journal of Gerontology*, 16:44, 1961.
Feifel, Herman. "The function of attitudes toward death". *Group for the Advancement of Psychiatry*, 5:632-641, October, 1965.
Feifel, Herman. "Is death's sting sharper for the doctor?". *Medical World News*, 8:77, October 6, 1967.
Feifel, Herman. "Older persons look at death". *Geriatrics*, 11:127-130, 1956.
Feifel, Herman. "The problem of death". *Catholic Psychological Record*, 3:18-22, 1965.
Feifel, Herman. "Scientific research in taboo areas - death". *American Behavioral Scientist*, 5:28-30, 1962.
Feifel, Herman. "The taboo on death". *The American Behavioral Scientist*, 6:66-67, May, 1963.
Feifel, Herman and Allan B. Branscomb. "Who's afraid of death?". *Journal of Abnormal Psychology*, 81(3):282-288, 1973.
Feifel, Herman, Jeffry Freilich and Lawrence J. Hermann. "Death fear in dying heart and cancer patients". *Journal of Psychosomatic Research*, 17(3):161-166, 1973.
Feigenberg, Loma. "Care and understanding of the dying patient - a patient centered approach". *Omega, Journal of Death and Dying*, 6(2):81-94, Spring, 1975.
Feldman, M.J. and M. Hersen. "Attitudes toward death in nightmare subjects". *Journal of Abnormal Psychology*, 72:421-425, 1967.
Fellner, C.H. and S.H. Schwartz. "Altruism in disrepute. Medical versus public attitudes toward the living organ donor". *New England Journal of Medicine*, 284:582-585, 1971.
Felner, Robert D., Arnold Stolberg, and Emory L. Cowen. "Crisis events and school mental health referral patterns of young children". *Journal of Consulting and Clinical Psychology*, 43(3):305-310, June, 1975.

Ferber, Max. "I cried but not for Irma". *Reader's Digest*, 108(648):92-94, April, 1976.
Ferenczi, Sandor. "The unwelcome child and his death-instinct". *International Journal of Psychoanalysis*, 10:125, 1929.
Ferkiss, Victor. "Facing up to the inescapable". *Commonweal*, 101(8):216-217, November 29, 1974.
Fermaglich, Joseph H. "Determining cerebral death". *American Family Physician*, 3(3):85-87, 1971.
Fischoff, J. and N. O'Brien. "After the child dies". *Journal of Pediatrics*, 88:140-146, January, 1976.
Fisher, Gary. "Death, identity and creativity". *Omega: Journal of Death and Dying*, 2:303-306, 1971.
Fisher, Gary. "Psychotherapy for the dying: principles and illustrative cases with special references to the use of LSD". *Omega: Journal of Death and Dying*, 1:3-15, 1970.
Fishers, Jean Ruth. "The nursing care of terminally ill patients". *Nursing Research*, 92, 1966.
Flannery, Raymond B., Jr. "Behavior modification of geriatric grief: a transactional perspective". *The International Journal of Aging and Human Development*, 5(2):197-203, 1974.
Fleming, J. and S. Altschul. "Activation of mourning and growth by psychoanalysis". *International Journal of Psychoanalysis*, 44:419-431, 1963.
Fleming, Joan and Sol Altschul. "Activation of mourning growth by psychoanalysis". *Bulletin of the Philadelphia Association of Psychoanalysts*, 9:37-38, 1959.
Fletcher, J. "The patient's right to die". *Harper's*, 221:141, October, 1960.
Fletcher, Joseph. "Ethics and euthanasia". *American Journal of Nursing*, 73:670-5, April, 1973.
Flinchum, G.A. "Death registration practices and problems". *North Carolina Medical Journal*, 29:176-177, April, 1968.
Flugel, J.C. "Death instinct, homeostasis and allied concepts". *International Journal of Psychoanalysis*, (Supplement). 34:43-74, 1953.
Fodor, N. "Jung's sermons to the dead". *Psychoanalytic Review*, 51:74-78, 1964.
Folck, Marilyn Melcher and Phyllis J. Nie. "Nursing students learn to face death". *Nursing Outlook*, 7:510-513, 1959.

Follett, E. "No time for fear". *Canadian Nursing Journal*, 66:39-40, January, 1970.

Folta, Jeannette R. "The perception of death". *Nursing Research*, 14:232-235, Summer, 1965.

Fontenot, Christine. "The subject nobody teaches". *English Journal*, 63:62-63, 1974.

Ford, A.B. "Casualties of our time". *Science*, 167:256-263, January 16, 1970.

Forest, Jack D. "The major emphasis of the funeral". *Pastoral Psychology*, 14:19-24, 1963.

Formanek, Ruth. "When children ask about death," *Elementary School Journal*, (November 1974), pp. 92-97.

Foster, L.E., Erich Lindemann and Rollin J. Fairbanks. "Grief". *Pastoral Psychology*, 1:28-30, 1950.

Foster, Zelda. "How social work can influence management of fatal illness". *Social Work*, 10(4):30-35, 1965.

Fox, Jeane E. "Reflections on cancer nursing". *American Journal of Nursing*, 66:1317-1319, June, 1966.

Foxe, A.N. "Criticue of Freud's concept of a death instinct". *Psychoanalytic Review*, 30:417-427, 1943.

Frake, Charles. "The diagnosis of disease among the subanum of Mindarao". *American Anthropologist*, 63:113-132, 1963.

Francis, Gloria M. "Cancer: the emotional component". *American Journal of Nursing*, 69(8):1677-1681, August, 1969.

Frankl, Viktor E. "Psychiatry and man's quest for meaning". *Journal of Religion and Health*, 1:93-103, 1962.

Franzblau, Abraham and Gotthard Booth. "Physicians, clergymen and the hospitalized patient". *Journal of the American Medical Association*, 200:354-356, April 24, 1967.

Frederick, J.F. "The physiology of grief". *Dodge Magazine*, 63:8-10, 1971.

Frederick, Jerome F. "Grief and cancer (Article I)". *The Dodge Magazine*, 68(2):4-5, March, 1976.

Frederick, Jerome F. "Grief and cancer (Article II)". *The Dodge Magazine*, 68(3):4-5, June, 1976.

Freedman, Ronald, Lolagene C. Coombs, and Judith Friedman. "Social correlates of fetal mortality". *Milbank Memorial Fund Quarterly*, 44(3):327-344, July, 1966.

Freedman, A.R. "Interview the parents of a dead child? Absolutely". *Clinic of Pediatrics*, 8:564-565, October, 1969.

Freymann, John Gordon. "A doctor prescribes for the AMA". *Harper's*, 231(1383):76-80, August, 1965.

Friedlander, Kate. "On the 'longing to die'". *International Journal of Psychoanalysis*, 21:416-426, 1940.

Friedman, B. "Care of the family of the child with cancer". *Pediatrics*, 40(3):498-504, Pt. 2, 1967.

Friedman, D.B. "Death anxiety and the primal scene". *Psychoanalytic Review*, 48:108-119, 1961.

Friedman, Henry J. "Physician management of dying patients: an exploration". *Psychiatry in Medicine*, 1:295-305, 1970.

Friedman, J. "Paradoxical response to death of spouse". *Diseases of the Nervous System*, 25:480-485, 1964.

Friedman, Stanford B. et. al. "Behavioral observations of parents anticipating the death of a child". *Pediatrics*, 32:610-625, 1963.

Frilous, G. Anthony, Jr. "Death - when does it occur?". *Baylor Law Review*, 27(1):10, Winter, 1975.

Fritz, Mary Apolline. "A study of widowhood". *Sociology and Social Research*, 14:553-559, 1930.

Fujimori, B. "Standards of determining death. Cerebral death from the standpoint of neurophysiology". *Surgical Therapy*, 20:415-422, April, 1969.

Fulton, Robert. "Attitudes toward death - a discussion". *Journal of Gerontology*, 16:63-65, January, 1961.

Fulton, Robert. "The clergyman and the funeral director: a study in role conflict". *Social Forces*, 39:317-323, May, 1961.

Fulton, Robert. "Death and dying: some sociological aspects of terminal care". *Modern Medicine*, 40:74-77, May 29, 1972.

Fulton, Robert. "Death and the self". *Journal of Religion and Health*, 3:359-368, 1964.

Fulton, Robert. "Death, grief and social recuperation". *Omega*, 1:23-28, February, 1970.

Fulton, Robert and Eric Markusen. "Childhood bereavement and behavior disorders: a critical review". *Omega*, 2:107-117, May, 1971.

Fulton, Robert and Gilbert Geis. "Death and social values". *Indian Journal of Social Research*, 3:7-14, 1962.

Fulton, Robert and Gilbert Geis. "Social change and social conflict: the rabbi and the funeral director". *Sociological Symposium*, 1:1-9, Fall, 1968.

Fulton, Robert and Julie Fulton. "A psychosocial aspect of terminal care: anticipatory grief". *Omega: Journal of Death and Dying*, 2:91-100, 1971.

Fulton, Robert and Phyllis Langton. "Attitudes toward death: an emerging mental health problem". *Nursing Forum*, 3:104-112, 1964.

Fulton, Robert, Roberta Simmons and Julie Fulton. "The prospective organ transplant donor: problems and prospects of medical innovation". *Omega*, 3:319-39, November, 1972.

"Funerals: the sting". *Newsweek*, 83:88, April 15, 1974.

Galdston, Iago. "Eros and thantos: a critique and elaboration of Freud's death wish". *American Journal of Psychoanalysis*, 15:123-134, 1955.

Gallagher, Nora. "Why people kill themselves . . . and what we can do to keep the numbers down". *Today's Health*, 54:46-50, February, 1976.

Gardner, L. Pearl. "Attitudes and activities of the middle-aged and aged". *Geriatrics*, 1:33-50, January-February, 1944.

Gardner, M.J., M.D. Crawford and J.N. Morris. "Patterns of mortality in middle and early old age in the county boroughs of England and Wa es". *British Journal of Preventive Sociological Medicine*, 23:133-140, 1969.

Gartley, W. and M. Bernasconi. "The concept of death in children". *Journal of Genetic Psychology*, 110:71-85, March, 1967.

Gauthier, Y. "The mourning reaction of a ten-year-old boy". *Canadian Psychiatric Association Journal*, 11:307-308, 1966.

Gaylen, William. "Harvesting the dead". *Harper's*, 249(1492):23-40, September, 1974.

Gaynor, Mildred. "On facing death". *Nursing Outlook*, 7:509, September, 1959.

Gaynor, Mildred. "What man shall live and not see death?". *Nursing Outlook*, 12:23, January, 1964.

Geber, M. "The physician, the child and death. 2. The anguish of death during psychotherapy of children". *Revue de Medecine Psychosomatique et de Psychologie Medicale*, 10:419-423, October-December, 1968.

Gealy, Fred D. "The Biblical understanding of death". *Pastoral Psychology*, 14:33-40, 1963.

Geertz, Clifford. "Ritual and social change: a Javanese example". *American Anthropologist*, 59:32-54, 1957.

Geis, D.P. "Mothers' perceptions of care given their dying children". *American Journal of Nursing*, 65:105-107, January, 1965.

Gerber, Irwin. "Bereavement and the acceptance of professional service". *Community Mental Health Journal*, 5(6):487-495, 1969.

Gerber, Irwin et. al. "Anticipatory grief and aged widows and widowers". *Journal of Gerontology*, 30(2):225-229, 1975.

Geringer, Erich. "Fear of death". *Spectator*, 189:179-180, August 8, 1952.

Gerlach, J. "Brain death and total death". *Munchener Medizinische Wochenschrift*, 111:732-736, March 28, 1969.

Gerlach, J. "Syndromes of dying and bita reducta". *Munchener Medizinische Wochenschrift*, 111:169-176, January 24, 1969.

"Ghost stories". *Time*, 69(7):69-70, February 18, 1957.

Gibson, P.C. "The dying patient". *Practitioner*, 186:85-91, 1961.

Giesdorf, P. "Observations on cremations". *Zeitschrift fur die Gesamte Hygiene und Ihre Grenzgebiete*, 10:17-27, 1964.

Gifford, Sanford. "Death and forever: some fears of war and peace". *Atlantic Monthly*, 209:88-92, March, 1962.

Gillespie, W.H. "Some regressive phenomena in old age". *British Journal of Medical Psychology*, 36:203-209, 1963.

Gilli, R. et. al. "On the ascertainment of death and on freedom to remove organs for transplantation". *Minerva Anestesiologica*, 34:1340-1351, November, 1968.

Gillon, H. "Defining death anew: brains oxygen use". *Science News*, 95:50, January 11, 1969.

Ginsberg, R. "Should the elderly cancer patient be told?". *Geriatrics*, 4:101-107, 1949.

Glaser, Barney G. "The physician and the dying patient". *Medical Opinion and Review*, 1:108-114, December, 1965.

Glaser, Barney G. and Anselm L. Strauss. "Dying on time". *Trans-action*, 27-31, May-June, 1965.

Glaser, R. and A. Strauss. "Temporal aspects of dying as a nonscheduled status passage". *American Journal of Sociology*, 81:48-59, July, 1965.

Glidden, Thomas. "The American funeral". *Pastoral Psychology*, 14:9-18, 1963.

Goff, Willard F. "How can a physician prepare his patient for death". *Journal of the American Medical Association*, 201:280, July 24, 1967.

Goldberg, Stanley B. "Family tasks and reactions in the crisis of death". *Social Work*, 54(7):398-405, 1973.

Goldfarb, A.I. "Death and dying: attitudes of patients and doctor". *Group for the Advancement of Psychiatry: Symposium*, 5:591-606, October, 1965.

Goldstein, Eda G. "Social casework and the dying person". *Social Casework*, 54(10):601-608, 1973.

Goldstein, S. "Jewish mortality and survival patterns: Providence, Rhode Island, 1962-1964". *Eugenics Quarterly*, 13:48-61, March, 1966.

Golding, Stephen L., George E. Atwood and Richard A. Goodman. "Anxiety and two cognitive forms of resistance to the idea of death". *Psychological Reports*, 18:359-364, 1966.

"Good death". *Time*, 105(10):83-84, March 10, 1975.

Goodman, David. "When a loved one dies". *The Boston Traveler*, Tuesday, March 9, 1965. p. 35.

Goodman, J.M. et. al. "Determination of brain death by isotope angiography". *Journal of the American Medical Association*, 209:1869-1872, September 22, 1969.

Goody, Jack. "Death and social control among the Lo Dagaa". *Man*, 59:134-138, 1959b.

Goody, Jack. "Religion and ritual: the definitional problem". *British Journal of Sociology*, 12:142-164, 1961.

Gordon, Arthur. "Answer at nightfall". *Reader's Digest*, 97:143-145, September, 1970.

Gossage, H.L. "Tell me doctor, will I be active right up to the last?". *Atlantic Monthly*, 224:55-57, September, 1969.

Goth, Louis A. "The coldest man alive". *Reader's Digest*, 104(622):132-136, February, 1974.

Gough, E.K. "Cults of the dead among the Nayars". *Journal of American Folklore*, 71:446-478, 1958.

Gould, D. "Better way to die". *New Statesman*, 77:474-475, April 4, 1969.

Gould, D. "Right to die". *New Statesman*, 77:402, March 21, 1969.

Graham, J.B. "Acceptance of death - beginning of life". *North Carolina Medical Journal*, 24:317-319, 1963.

"Gramp's decision to die". *Today's Health*, 53(5):12, 1975.

Granville-Grossman, K.L. "Early bereavement and schizophrenia". *British Journal of Psychiatry*, 112:1027-1034, 1966.

Green, Patricia. "The child with leukemia in the classroom". *American Journal of Nursing*, 75(1):86-87, January, 1975.

Gregg, Gary. "Suicide: the Werther effect: following the famous suicides". *Psychology Today*, 8(5):28+, October, 1974.

Gregory, Ian. "Studies of parental deprivation in psychiatric patients". *American Journal of Psyciatry*, 115:432-442, 1958.

Green, M. and A.J. Solnit. "Psychologic considerations in the management of deaths on pediatric hospital services". pt. 1, "The doctor and the child's family". *Pediatrics*, 24:106-112, 1959.

Green, Morris. "Care of the dying child". *Pediatrics*, 40(3):492-497, Pt. 2, 1967.

Green, W.A. "Role of a vicarious object in the adaptation of object loss: I. Use of a vicarious object". *Psychosomatic Medicine*, 20:344-350, 1958.

Greenberg, Lois D. "Therapeutic grief work with children". *Social Casework*, 56(7):396-403, July, 1975.

Greenberg, N.H., John G. Loesch and Martin Lakin. "Life situations associated with the onset of pregnancy: I. The role of separation in a group of unmarried women". *Psychosomatic Medicine*, 21:291-311, 1959.

Greenberger, Ellen. "Fantasies of women confronting death". *Journal of Consulting Psychology*, 29:252-260, 1965.

Greenberger, Ellen. "'Flirting' with death: fantasies of a critically ill woman". *Journal of Projective Techniques*, 30:197-204, 1966.

Greenfeld, Josh A. "A dramatic sense of age . . . a sudden sniff of death". *Today's Health*, 51:44, 1973.

Greer, Ina May. "Grief must be faced". *Christian Century*, 62:269-271, 1945.

Gregory, I. "Retrospective estimates of orphanhood from generation life tables". *Milbank Memorial Fund Quarterly*, 43:323-348, 1965.

Griffin, Jerry. "Family decision: a crucial factor in terminating life". *American Journal of Nursing*, 75(5):794-796, May, 1975.

Grinberg, Leon. "Two kinds of guilt: their relationship with normal pathological aspects of mourning". *International Journal of Psychoanalysis*, 45:366-371, 1964.

Grollman, Earl A. "Counseling of the potential suicide". *Pastoral Psychology*, 20:187, January, 1966.

Grollman, Earl A. "Death and responsibility". *Psychiatric Opinion*, 3(6):36-38, December, 1966.

Grollman, Earl A. "Insights of psychiatry in understanding God". *American Imago*, 20:187, 1963.

Grollman, Earl A. "Pastoral counseling of the potential suicidal person". *Pastoral Psychology*, 16(160):46+, January, 1966.

Gross, Carol K. "My turn - death is a personal matter". *Newsweek*, 87(2):9, January 12, 1976.

Grossman, K.L. "Maternal age and parental loss". *British Journal of Psychiatry*, 114.242-243, February, 1968.

Grossman, Melvyn L. "The psychosocial approach to the medical management of patients with cystic fibrosis". *Clinical Pediatrics (Philadelphia)*, 14:830-833, September, 1975.

Grotjahn, Martin. "Ego identity and the fear of death and dying". *Hillside Hospital Journal*, 9:147-155, 1960.

Group for the Advancement of Psychiatry. "The right to die: decision and decision makers". *GAP Report*, 8:667-751, 1973.

Guerney, Edward. "Is there a right to die? A study of the law of euthanasia". *Cumberland-Samford Law Review*, 3:235, September, 1972.

Guiderauz, M. et. al. "General data on mortality statistics". *Bulletin de L'institut National de al Sante et de la Recher-Medicale*, 21:57-79, 1966.

Guimond, Joyce. "We knew our child was dying". *American Journal of Nursing*, 74(2):248-249, 1974.

Gunther, Jan. "How to survive widowhood". *Reader's Digest*, 106(638):181-186, June, 1975.

Gut, Emmy. "Some aspects of adult mourning". *Omega: Journal of Death and Dying*, 5(4):323-341, 1974.

Gutentag, Otto E. "The meaning of death in medical theory". *Stanford Medical Bulletin*, 17:165-170, August, 1959.

Guthrie, George P. "The meaning of death". *Omega: Journal of Death and Dying*, 2:299-302, 1971.

Gutmann, D. "The premature gerontocracy: themes of aging and death in the youth culture". *Social Research*, 39:416-448, 1972.

Guttentag, O. "The meaning of death in medical theory". *Stanford Medical Bulletin*, 17(4):165-170, 1959.

Gyulay, Jo-Eileen. "The forgotten grievers". *American Journal of Nursing*, 75:1476-1479, 1975.

Haas, Michael. "Toward the study of biopolitics: a cross-sectional analysis of mortality rates". *Behavioral Science*, 14(4):257-280, 1969.

Hackett, T.P. and A.D. Weisman. "Predilection to death: death and dying as a psychiatric problem". *Psychosomatic Medicine*, 23:232-256, May-June, 1961.

Hackett, Thomas P. and Avery D. Weisman. "The treatment of the dying". *Current Psychiatric Therapy*, 2:121-126, 1962.

Hackl, H. "Research on mortality during the course of the year". *Revue Lyonnaise de Medecine*, 14:10-14, 1965.

Haider, Ijaz. "Attitudes toward death of psychiatric patients". *International Journal of Neuropsychiatry*, 3(11):10-14, 1967.

Hall, Elizabeth and Paul Cameron. "Our failing reverence for life". *Psychology Today*, 9(11):104-108, April, 1976.

Hall, G.S. "A study of fears". *American Journal of Psychology*, 26:147-249, 1897.

Hall, G.S. "Thanatophobia and immortality". *American Journal of Psychology*, 26:550-613, 1915.

Hall, Robert E. "The gray zones of life". *Nation*, 221(14):421, November 1, 1975.

Hamner, R.T. "Legal death--can it be defined?". *Journal of the Medical Association of Alabama*, 38:610-614, January, 1969.

Hammond, E.C. "Smoking in relation to the death rates of one million men and women". *National Cancer Institute Monographs*, 19:127-204, January, 1966.

Handal, P.J. "The relationship between subjective life expectancy, death anxiety and general anxiety". *Journal of Clinical Psychology*, 25:39-42, 1969.

Handal, Paul J. "Relationship between the death anxiety scale and repression". *Journal of Clinical Psychology*, 31:675-677, October, 1975.

Hankoff, L.D. "Adolescence and the crisis of dying". *Adolescence*, 10(39):373-386, Fall, 1975.
Hankoff, L.D. "Suicide prevention service". *Medical Tribune*, 5(116): _____ , October 28, 1964.
Hansen, G. "Diagnosis of death, reanimation organ transplantation". *Zeitschrift fur Aerztliche Fortbildung,* 63:237-239, February 15, 1969.
Harbison, Janet. "New patterns for American funerals". *Presbyterian Life*, 8+, August 1, 1964.
Hardgrove, Carol and Louise H. Warrick. "How shall we tell the children?". *American Journal of Nursing*, 74(3):448-450, 1974.
Hardt, Dale V. "A measurement of the improvement of attitudes toward death". *The Journal of School Health*, 46(5):269-270, 1976.
Hardt, Dale. "Development of an investigatory instrument to measure attitudes toward death". *Journal of School Health*, 45(2), February, 1975.
Harmetz, Aljean. "How to beat the funeral industry". *Pageant*, 68-74, May, 1964.
Harnik, J. "One component of the fear of death in early infancy". *International Journal of Psychoanalysis*, 11:485-491, 1930.
Harris, Elisabeth T. "On giving oneself away". *Harper's*, 229(1375):99-101, December, 1964.
Harris, Martha. "The complexity of mental pa n seen in a six-year old child following sudden bereavement". *Journal of Child Psychotherapy*, 3:35-45, 1973.
Hatt, H.E. "Mystery of death and the problem of transplants". *The Christian Century*, 86:441-444, April 2, 1969.
Heckel, R.V. "The day the President was assassinated: patient's reaction in one mental hospital". *Mental Hospitals*, 15:48, 1964.
Heilbrum, Gert. "The basic fear". *Journal of the American Psychoanalytic Association*, 3:447-466, 1955.
Heilig, Sam M. "Training in suicide prevention". *Bulletin of Suicidology*, 6:41-44, Spring, 1970.
Heilig, Sam M. et. al. "The role of non-professional volunteers in a suicide prevention center". *Community Mental Health*, 4(4):287-295, 1968.

Heinicke, C.M. "Some effects of separating two-year-old children from their parents: a comparative study". *Human Relations*, 9:105-176, 1956.

Heinz, W.C. "The man who said they don't have to die". *Today's Health*, 49(1):26-29+, January, 1971.

Hembright, T.Z. "Comparison of information on death certificates and matching 1960 census records: age, marital status, race, nativity and country of origin". *Demography*, 6:413-423, 1969.

Hendal, P.J. "The relationship between subjective life expectancy, death anxiety and general anxiety". *Journal of Clinical Psychology*, 25:39-42, 1969.

Hendin, David. "Death as a fact of life". *Science Digest*, 73(6):34-39, June, 1973.

Henrickson, Sharon. "A philosophy of death made personal". *American Journal of Nursing*, 76(1):90, January, 1976.

Hershey, N. "Questions of life and death". *American Journal of Nursing,* 68:1910-1912, September, 1968.

Hertzberg, Leonard. "Cancer and the dying patient". *American Journal of Psychiatry*, 128:806-810, 1972.

Herxheimer, H. "Sudden death in a young asthmatic". *British Medical Journal*, 2:246, April 26, 1969.

Heyman, D. and D.T. Gianturco. "Long-term adaptation by the elderly to bereavement". *Journal of Gerontology*, 28(3):359-362, 1973.

Heyman, D.A. "Discussions meet needs of dying patients". *Hospitals, Journal of the American Hospital Association*, 48:57-62, July 16, 1974.

Hickerson, Harold. "The feast of the dead among the seventeenth century Alonquians of the Upper Great Lakes". *American Anthropologist*, 62:81-107, 1960.

Hicks, William and Robert S. Daniels. "The dying patient, his physician and the psychiatric consultant". *Psychosomatics*, 9:47-52, January-February, 1968.

Hilgard, J.R. "Depressive and psychotic states as anniversaries to sibling death in childhood". *International Psychiatry Clinics*, 6:197, 1969.

Hilgard, Josephine R. "Anniversary reactions in parents precipitated by children". *Psychiatry*, 16:73-80, 1953.

Hilgard, Josephine R. and Fern Fisk. "Disruption of adult ego identity as related to childhood loss of a mother through hospitalization for psychosis". *The Journal of Nervous and Mental Disease*, 131:47-57, July, 1969.

Hilgard, Josephine R. and M.F. Newman. "Anniversaries in mental illness". *Psychiatry*, 22:113-121, 1959.

Hilgard, Josephine R. and M.F. Newman. "Early parental deprivation in schizophrenia and alcoholism". *American Journal of Orthopsychiatry*, 33:409-420, 1963.

Hilgard, Josephine R. and M.F. Newman. "Evidence for functional genesis in mental illness: schizophrenia, depressive psychoses and psychoneuroses". *The Journal of Nervous and Mental Disease*, 132:3-16, January, 1961.

Hilgard, Josephine R. and M.F. Newman. "Parental loss by death in childhood as an etiological factor among schizophrenic and alcoholic patients compared with a non-patient community sample". *Journal of Nervous and Mental Disease*, 137:14-28, 1963.

Hilgard, Josephine R., M.F. Newman and F. Fisk. "Strength of adult ego following childhood bereavement". *American Journal of Orthopsychiatry*, 30:788-798, 1960.

Hill, David S. "How to plan your own funeral". *Reader's Digest*, 107(642):61-64, October, 1975.

Hill, O.W. and J.S. Price. "Childhood bereavement and adult depression". *British Journal of Psychiatry*, 113:743-751, 1967.

Hill, Oscar V. "The association of childhood bereavement with suicidal attempt in depressive illness". *British Journal of Psychiatry*, 115:301-304, 1969.

Hinton, J.M. "Facing death". *Journal of Psychosomatic Research*, 10:22-28, 1966.

Hinton, J.M. "The physical and mental distress of the dying". *Quarterly Journal of Medicine*, 32:1-21, 1963.

Hinton, J.M. "Problems in the care of the dying". *Journal of Chronic Diseases*, 17:201-205, 1961.

Hinton, John. "Assessing the views of the dying". *Social Science and Medicine*, 5:37-43, 1971.

Hirsch, J. "Suicide (Part 5: the trouble shooting clinic: prototype of a comprehensive community emergency service)". *Mental Hygiene*, 44:496-502, 1960.

Hobbins, William B. "Four distinctive views of the dying patient: what is a day of life worth?". *RN*, 38(4):33-34, 1975.

Hofer, G. "Death in the primitive world (on the question of death suggestion in Melanesia)". *Confinia Psychiatrica*, 9:93-114, 1966.

Hoffman, Esther. "Don't give up on me". *American Journal of Nursing*, 71(1):60-62, January, 1971.

Hoffman, Francis H. and Morris W. Brody. "The symptom: fear of death". *Psychoanalytic Review*, 44:433-438, 1957.

Hoffman, Frederick J. and J. Grace. "Violence and self". *Virginia Quarterly Review*, 34:439-454, 1958.

Hoffman, James W. "When a loved one is dying. . .". *Today's Health*, 50(2):41-43, 1972.

Hofling, Charles K. "Terminal decisions". *Medical Opinion and Review*, 2(1):40-49, October, 1966.

Hollis, James. "The relevance of death". *The Chronicle of Higher Education*, 20:24, May 27, 1975.

Holmes, T.H. and R.H. Rahe. "The social readjustment rating scale". *Journal of Psychosomatic Research*, 11:213-218, 1967.

Holt, William C. "Death by suggestion". *Canadian Psychiatric Association Journal*, 14:81-82, 1969.

"Home to the heartland". *Time*, 93:26-27, April 11, 1969.

Horn, Jack. "The dying child pushes parents away". *Psychology Today*, 8:30, April, 1975.

Horn, Jack. "Life and death, a different approach to the dying patient". *Psychology Today*, 9(2):88, 1975.

Horn, Jack. "Violence: the misunderstood matters of suicide". *Psychology Today*, 8(7):138, December, 1974.

Horn, Patrice. "Death - dealing with the dying child". *Psychology Today*, 8(11):29-30, April, 1975.

Horwitz, Julius. "This is the age of the aged". *The New York Times*, 82-86, May, 1965.

"How kids look at death". *Science Digest*, 72(2):24-25, September, 1972.

Howard, Alan and Robert A. Scott. "Cultural values and attitudes toward death". *Journal of Existentialism*, 6:161-174, 1965-1966.

Howard, Elaine. "The effect of work experience on the attitudes toward death held by nurse aides". *Gerontologist*, 14(1):54-56, 1974.

Howard, J.D. "Fear of death". *Journal of the Indiana Medical Association*, 54:1773-1779, 1961.
Howard, T. "Human experience of death". *Christianity Today*, 14:6-3, November 21, 1969.
Howell, D.A. "A child dies". *Hospital Topics*, 45:93-96, February, 1967.
Howell, Milton M. "The Lone Eagle's last flight". *Journal of the American Medical Association*, 232(7):715, 1975.
Howie, D L. "Scared to death". *Journal of the Florida Medical Association*, 55:861-862, September, 1968.
Human, Mildred E. "Death of a neighbor". *American Journal of Nursing*, 73:1914-1916, November, 1973.
Hummel, Robert. "Death with dignity legislation". *Hospital Progress*, 57(6):50-58, 1976.
Inamoto, A. "Standards for determining death. Cerebral death from the standpoint of anesthesiology". *Surgical Therapy*, 20:427-432, April, 1969.
Ingles, T. "Death on a ward". *Nursing Outlook*, 12:28, 1964.
"Integrity death". *Integrity*, March, 1956.
Irion, Paul E. "The funeral and the integrity of the church". *Pastoral Psychology*, 14:25-32, 1963.
Irion, Paul E. "The future of the funeral". *The Mid-Continent Mortician*, 10-12, December, 1966.
Irion, Paul E. "In the midst of life . . . death!". *Pastoral Psychology*, 14:7-14, June, 1963.
Irwin, Robert and Donald L. Weston. "Preschool child's response to death of an infant sibling". *American Journal of Diseases of Children*, 106(6):564-567, December, 1963.
"Is God dead?". *Time*, 93:44, May 2, 1969.
"Isolation and the dying child". *Science Digest*, 77(4):24-25, April, 1975.
Jablon, S. et. al. "Studies of the mortality of A-Bomb survivors". *Radiation Research*, 25:25-52, 1965.
Jackson, Edgar N. "Grief and depression (Part 2)". *The Dodge Magazine*, 68(1):9+, January, 1976.
Jackson, Edgar N. "Grief and depression (Part 3)". *The Dodge Magazine*, 68(2):13+, March, 1976.
Jackson, Edgar N. "Grief and guilt". *The Pastoral Counselor*, 1:34-38, Spring, 1963.

Jackson, Edgar N. "Grief and humor (Part 3)". *The Dodge Magazine*, 67(1):21, 28, January, 1975.
Jackson, Edgar N. "Grief and self-deceit (Part 2)". *The Dodge Magazine*, 67(3):9+, June, 1975.
Jackson, Edgar N. "Grief and self-deceit (Part 3)". *The Dodge Magazine*, 67(4):14+, September, 1975.
Jackson, Edgar N. "Grief and self-deceit (Part 4)". *The Dodge Magazine*, 67(2):20+, March, 1975.
Jackson, Edgar N. "Grief and self-punishment (Part I)". *The Dodge Magazine*, 68(3):25+, June, 1976.
Jackson, Maurice. "The Black experience with death: a brief analysis through black writings". *Omega: Journal of Death and Dying*, 3(3):203-209, 1972.
Jackson, Pat Ludder. "Chronic grief". *American Journal of Nursing*, 74:1288-1291, 1974.
Jackson, Pat Ludder. "The child's developing concept of death: implications of nursing care of the terminally ill child". *Nursing Forum*, 14(2):204-215, 1975.
Jacobs, J.L. "Spiritual resources for the aged in facing the problem of death". *Bulletin of the Institute of Gerontology*, Supplement 3, 6:3-8, 1950.
Jacques, Elliott. "Death and the mid-life crisis". *International Journal of Psychoanalysis*, 46:506-512, 1965.
Jakobovits, I. "The dying and their treatment in Jewish law". *Hebrew Medical Journal*, 2:242-251, 1961.
James, T.N. "QT prolongation and sudden death". *Modern Concepts in Cardiovascular Disease*, 38:34-37, July, 1969.
Jeffers, Frances C., C.R. Nichols, and C. Eisdorfer. "Attitudes of older persons toward death: a preliminary study". *Journal of Gerontology*, 16:53-56, 1961.
Jelliffe, S.E. "The death instinct in somatic and psychopathology". *Psychoanalytic Review*, 20:121-131, 1933.
Jensen, Gordon D. and John G. Wallace. "Family mourning process". *Family Process*, 6:56-66, 1967.
Jha, M. "Death rites among Maithil Brahmans". *Man in India*, 46(3):241-247, 1966.
Jinnal, D. "Standards for determining death. Death from the standpoint of the surgeon". *Surgical Therapy*, 20:409-414, April, 1969.

Johannsen, Dorothea E. "Reactions to the death of President Roosevelt". *Journal of Abnormal and Social Psychology*, 41:218-222, 1946.

Johnson, Beverley H. "Before hospitalization: a preparation program for the child and his family". *Children Today*, 18-21, November-December, 1974.

Johnson, W.G. "To die as a man: disease, truth and Christian ethics". *Journal of the Iowa Medical Society*, 56:813-816, August, 1966.

Johnston, E.H. et. al. "Investigation of sudden death in addicts, with emphasis on the toxicological findings in thirty cases". *Medical Annals of the District of Columbia*, 38:375-380, July, 1969.

Jones, Christine H. "Four distinctive views of the dying patient: a kidney donor: providing life after death". *RN*, 38(4):36-37, 1975.

Jones, K.S "Death and doctors". *Medical Journal of Australia*, 49:329-334, 1962.

Jones, Sara M. "The magic room". *Good Housekeeping*, 171:83+, December, 1973.

Jones, T.T. "Dignity in death. The application and withholding of interventive measures". *Journal of the Louisiana Medical Society*, 13:180-183, 1961.

Jonkman, E.J. "Cerebral death and the isoelectric EEG". *Electroencephalography and Clinical Neurophysiology*, 27:215, August, 1969.

Joseph, F. "Transference and Counter-transference in the case of a dying patient". *Psychoanalysis*, 49:21-34, 49:21-34, 1962.

Jury, Mark. "The nobility of our Gramp's decision to die". *Today's Health*, 53(1):18-23, 1975.

Jury, Mark and Dan. "Gramp". *Psychology Today*, 9(9):57-63, February, 1976.

Kahana, Boaz and Eva. "Attitudes of young men and women toward awareness of death". *Omega: Journal of Death and Dying*, 3:37-44, 1972.

Kalish, R.A. "The practicing physician and death research". *Medical Times*, 97:211-220, January, 1969.

Kalish, Richard A. "The aged and the dying process: the inevitable decisions". *Journal of Social Issues*, 21:87-96, 1965.

Kalish, Richard A. "An approach to the study of death attitudes". *American Behavioral Scientist*, 6:68-70, 1963.

Kalish, Richard A. "A continuum of subjectively perceived death". *Gerontologist*, 6:73-76, 1966.

Kalish, Richard A. "Dealing with the grieving family". *RN*, 26:81-84, 1963.

Kalish, Richard A. "Death and responsibility: a social-psychological view". *Psychiatric Opinion*, 3(4):14-19, August, 1966.

Kalish, Richard A. "Of social values and the dying: a defense of disengagement". *The Family Coordinator*, 21(1):81-94, 1972.

Kalish, Richard A. "Social distance and the dying". *Community Mental Health Journal*, 2:152-155, Summer, 1966.

Kalish, Richard A. "Some variables in death attitudes". *Journal of Social Psychology*, 59:137-145, 1963.

Kalish, Richard A. and David K. Reynolds. "Widows view death; a brief research note". *Omega: Journal of Death and Dying*, 5(2):187-192, 1974.

Kalsey, Virginia. "As life ebbs". *American Journal of Nursing*, 48:170-173, 1948.

Kane, Hermine. "Nursing - the end". *The American Mercury*, 19:458-461, April, 1930.

Kanoti, George. "Doctor, death and dying". *Linacre Quarterly*, 42(4):262-267, 1975.

Kaphan, M.N. and R.E. Litman. "Telephone appraisal of 100 suicidal emergencies". *American Journal of Psychotherapy*, 16(4):591-599, 1962.

Kaphan, Marvin N. and R.E. Litman. "Suicide consultation: a psychiatric service to social agencies". *American Journal of Psychiatry*, 122:1357-1361, June, 1966.

Kass, L.R. "Death as an event". *Science*, 173:698-702, 1972.

Kast, Eric. "LSD and the dying patient". *Chicago Medical School Quarterly*, 26:80-87, Summer, 1966.

Kastenbaum, Robert. "Death as a research problem in social gerontology: an overview". *Gerontologist*, 7:67-69, 1966.

Kastenbaum, R. "Kingdom where nobody dies". *Saturday Review*, 55(52):33-38, December 23, 1972.

Kastenbaum, R. "Multiple perspectives on a geriatric death valley". *Community Mental Health Journal*, 3:21-29, 1967.

Kastenbaum, R. and L. Briscoe. "The street corner: a laboratory for the study of life-threatening behavior". *Omega: Journal of Death and Dying*, 6(1):33-44, 1975.

Kastenbaum, Robert. "As the clock runs out". *Mental Hygiene*, 50:332-336, July, 1966.

Kastenbaum, Robert. "Death and responsibility: introduction" and "A critical review". *Psychiatric Opinion*, 3(4):5-6, 35-41, 1966.

Kastenbaum, Robert. "The mental health specialist and the American death system". *Psychiatric Opinion*, 9:28-37, 1972.

Kastenbaum, Robert. "On the future of death: some images and options". *Omega: Journal of Death and Dying*, 3:306-318, 1972.

Kastenbaum, Robert. "On the meaning of time in later life". *Journal of Genetic Psychology*, 109:9-25, 1966.

Kastenbaum, Robert. "The realm of death: an emerging area in psychological research". *Journal of Human Relations*, 13:538-552, 1965.

Kastenbaum, Robert and Charles E. Goldsmith. "The funeral director and the meaning of death". *American Funeral Director*, 86:35-37, April, 1963; 86:47-48, May, 1963; 86:45-46, June, 1963.

Kastenbaum, Robert and Ronald Koenig. "Dying, death and lethal behavior: an experience in community education". *Omega: Journal of Death and Dying*, 1:29-36, 1970.

Katz, Alfred H. "Who shall survive?". *Medical Opinion and Review*, 3(3):52-62, March, 1967.

Katz, Robert L. "Counseling the bereaved". *Central Conference of American Rabbis Yearbook*, 63:465-469, 1953.

Kaufer, C. et. al. "Time of death determination following dissociated death of the brain. Clinical and electroencelpholographic criteria". *Deutsche Medizinische Wochenschrift*, 93:679-684, April 5, 1968.

Kavanaugh, Robert E. "Helping patients who are facing death". *Nursing*, 4(5):35-42, May, 1974.

Kazamias, T.M. "What death is like". *American Heart Journal*, 78:139-140, July, 1969.

Keebler, Nancy. "When a child might die". *National Observer*, 1975.

Keiffer, Elisabeth. "A dying mother's plea for her children". *Good Housekeeping*, 181(1):56+, July, 1975.

Kelly, W.D. and S.R. Friesen. "Do cancer patients want to be told?". *Surgery*, 27:822, 1950.

Kelly, Wanda. "Until tomorrow comes". *Guideposts*, 2-6, April, 1976.

Kelly, William H. "Cocopa attitudes and practices with respect to death and mourning". *Southwestern Journal of Anthropology*, 5:151-164, 1949.

Kennard, E.A. "Hopi reactions to death". *American Anthropologist*, 29:491-494, 1937.

Kennell, John, Howard Slyter and Marshall H. Klaus. "The mourning response of parents to the death of a newborn infant". *Child and Family*, 9:221-230, 1970.

Kent, Saul. "Enlist now in the war on death". *Cavalier*, :36-38, March, 1967.

Kephart, William M. "Status after death". *American Sociological Review*, 15:635-643, 1950.

Kerenyi, Fekete. "Sudden unexpected death in infancy". *Canadian Journal of Public Health*, 60:357+, September, 1969.

Kevorkian, J. "The eye of death". *Clinical Symposia*, 13:51-62, 1961.

Keyes, E.L. "The fear of death". *Harper's Magazine*, 99:208-212, 1909.

Keyser, Cassius J. "The significance of death". *The Hibbert Journal*, 12:886, 1914.

Kidorf, Irwin W. "Jewish tradition and the Freudian theory of mourning". *Journal of Religion and Health*, 2:248-252, 1963.

Kidorf, Irwin W. "The shiva: a form of group psychotherapy". *Journal of Religion and Health*, 1:43-46, January, 1966.

Kiester, Edwin, Jr. "Six generations of one family linked together by a deadly gene". *Today's Health*, 54(3):32-35, March, 1976.

Kikuchi, June. "A leukemic adolescent's verbalization about dying". *Maternal-child Nursing Journal*, 1:259-264, 1972.

Killian, Eldon C. "Effect of geriatric transfers on mortality rates". *Social Work*, 15:19-26, January, 1970.

Kimsey, Larry R. et. al. "Death, dying and denial in the aged". *American Journal of Psychiatry*, 129:161-166, 1972.

Kimura, J. et. al. "The isoelectric electroencephalogram. Significance in establishing death in patients maintained on mechanical respirators". *Archives of Internal Medicine*, 121:511-517, June, 1968.

Kirkpatrick, Jeanne, et. al. "Bereavement and school adjustment". *Journal of School Psychology*, 3:58-63, 1965.

Kinkead, Eugene. "Is there another life after death?". *Look*, 34(21):84-90, October 20, 1970.

Kirtley, Donald D. and Joseph M. Sacks. "Reactions of a psychotherapy group to ambiguous circumstances surrounding the death of a group member". *Journal of Consulting and Clinical Psychology*, 33:195-199, 1969.

Kitay, William. "Let's retain the dignity of dying". *Today's Health*, 44:62-69, May. 1966.

Klebba, A.J. "Mortality trends in the United States". *Vital Health Statistics*, 20:1-57, June, 1966.

Klein, M. "Mourning and its relation to manic-depressive states". *International Journal of Psychoanalysis*, 21:125-153, 1940.

Klein, Melanie. "A contribution to the theory of anxiety and guilt". *International Journal of Psychoanalysis*, 29(114):114-123, 1948.

Kliman, Ann S. "Children, death and dying". *The Dodge Magazine*, 67(1):3, January, 1975.

Kluckhohn, Clyde. "Myths and rituals: a general theory". *Harvard Theological Review*, 35:45-79, 1942.

Klugman, David J., Robert E. Titman, and Carl Wald. "Suicide: answering cry for help". *Social Work*, 19(4):43-50, 1965.

Knight, Aldrich C. "Personality factors and mortality in the relocation of the aged". *The Gerontologist*, 4:92-93, 1964.

Knight, James A. "Philosophic implications of terminal illness". *North Carolina Medical Journal*, 22:493-495, 1961.

Knudson, Alfred G., Jr. and Joseph M. Natterson. "Observations concerning fear of death in fatally ill children and their mothers". *Psychosomatic Medicine*, 22(6):456-465, November-December, 1960.

Knudson, Alfred G. and Joseph M. Natterson. "Participation of parents in the hospital care of fatally ill children". *Pediatrics*, 26:482-490, 1960.

Knudson, Alfred G., Jr. and Joseph M. Natterson. "Practice of pediatrics - participation of parents in the hospital care of fatally ill children". *Pediatrics*, 26(3, pt. 1):482-490, September, 1960.

Kobrzycki, Paula. "Dying with dignity at home". *American Journal of Nursing*, 75(8): 1312-1313, August, 1975.

Koenig, Ronald. "Dying vs. well-being". *Omega: Journal of Death and Dying*, 4(3):181-194, 1973.

Koenigsberg, R.A. "F. Scott Fitzgerald: literature and the work of mourning". *American Imago*, 24:248-270, 1967.

Koestenbaum, Peter. "Aspects of death and dying. Philosophy: outlines of an existential theory of neuroses". *Journal of the American Medical Women's Association*, 14(6):472-488, June, 1964.

Koestenbaum, Peter. "The vitality of death". *Omega: Journal of Death and Dying*, 2:253-271, 1971.

Kohlhaas, M. "On the determination of the time of death of the deceased". *Deutsche Medizinische Wochenschrift*, 93:412-414, March, 1968.

Kohlhaas, M. "Once again: on determination of the time of death". *Deutsche Medizinische Wochenschrift*, 93:1575, August, 1968.

Kohn, Lawrence A. "Thoughts on the care of the hopelessly ill". *Medical Times*, 89:1177-1181, 1961.

Koocher, Gerald P. "Childhood, death and cognitive development". *Developmental Psychology*, 9:369-375, 1973.

Koocher, Gerald P. "Why isn't the gerbil moving anymore? Discussing death in the classroom - and at home". *Children Today*, 18-21, January-February, 1975.

Kopel, Kenneth et. al. "A human relations laboratory approach to death and dying". *Omega: Journal of Death and Dying*, 6:219-221, 1975.

Korkfors, G. et. al. "Parity and age of death". *Annales Chirurgiae et Gynaecologiae Fenniae*, 53:476-479, 1964.

Kostrubala, T. "Therapy of the terminally ill patient". *Illinois Medical Journal*, 124:545-547, 1963.

Koupernik, C. "A drama of our times: euthanasia". *Concours Medical*, 84:2687-2688, 1962.

Kowet, Don. "Never say die". *Today's Health*, 52:20, July, 1974.

Krahn, John H. "Pervasive death: an avoided concept". *Educational Leadership*, 31:18-20, 1973.

Kramer, Charles H. and Hope E. Dunlop. "The dying patient". *Geriatric Nursing*, 2:15+, September-October, 1966.

Krant, Melvin. "Dying: a meaningful summation of life". *Medical Insight*, 5(1):26-29, January, 1973.

Krant, Melvin A. "A death in the family". *Journal of the American Medical Association*, 231(2):195-196, January 13, 1975.

Kraus, Arthur and Abraham Lilenfeld. "Some epidemiologic aspects of the high mortality rate in the young widowed group". *Journal of Chronic Diseases*, 10:207-217, 1959.

Kravitz, H. et. al. "Death in suburbia". *Clinical Pediatrics*, 5:266-267, May, 1966.

Kretschmer, H. "Determination of the time of death from the neurosurgical viewpoint". *Zeitschrift fur Aerzliche Fortbildung*, 63:884-885, August 15, 1969.

Krieger, G.W. and Basque, L.O. "Terminal illness: counseling with a family perspective". *Family Coordinator*, 24(3):351-355, July, 1975.

Krippner, Stanley. "The 20-year death cycle of the American President". *Research Journal of Philosophy and Social Sciences*, 2:65-72, 1965.

Krisher, B. "Praying for death; elderly Japanese worshippers seeking good deaths". *Newsweek*, 87:10, February 16, 1976.

Kroeber, A.L. "Disposal of the dead". *American Anthropologist*, 26:308-315, 1927.

Kron, Joan. "Learning to live with death". *Omega: Journal of Death and Dying*, 5(1):5-24, 1974.

Krupp, G.R. "Notes on identification as a defense against anxiety in coping with loss". *International Journal of Psychoanalysis*, 46:303, 1963.

Krupp, George. "Maladaptive reactions to the death of a family member". *Social Casework*, 53(7):425-434, 1972.

Krupp, George R. and Bernard Kligfel. "The bereavement reaction: a cross-cultural evaluation". *Journal of Religion and Health*, 1:222-245, 1962.

Kubler-Ross, Elisabeth. "Anger before death". *Nursing*, 1(2):12-14, December, 1971.

Kubler-Ross, Elisabeth. "The care of the dying: whose job is it?". *Psychiatry in Medicine*, 1(2):103-107, April, 1970.

Kubler-Ross, Elisabeth. "Dignity in death". *Medical Bulletin, Naval Regional Medical Center and Naval Hospital, Portsmouth, Virginia*, 6(4):76-85, Winter, 1971.

Kubler-Ross, Elisabeth. "Dying from the patient's point of view". *Triangle, Sandoz Journal of Medical Science*, 13(1):25-26, 1974.

Kubler-Ross, Elisabeth. "The dying patient as teacher: an experiment and an experience". *Chicago Theological Seminary Register*, 57(3):1-14, December, 1966.

Kubler-Ross, Elisabeth. "Dying with dignity". *The Canadian Nurse*, 67(10):31-35, October, 1971.

Kubler-Ross, Elisabeth. "Elisabeth Kubler-Ross on death and dying. Help for the dying and their survivors". *Practical Psychology for Physicians*, 3:13-14+, February, 1976.

Kubler-Ross, Elisabeth. "Facing up to death; terminally ill patients". *Today's Education*, 61:30-32, January, 1972.

Kubler-Ross, Elisabeth. "The family physician and the dying patient". *Canadian Family Physician*, 79-83, October, 1972.

Kubler-Ross, Elisabeth. "How the patient faces death". *Public Welfare*, 29(1):56-60, January, 1971.

Kubler-Ross, Elisabeth. "Interview with terminal cancer patient". *Geratric Focus*, 9(4): _____, April, 1970.

Kubler-Ross, Elisabeth. "The languages of the dying patients". *Humanitas*, 10(1):5-8, February, 1974.

Kubler-Ross, Elisabeth. "Letter to a nurse about death". *Nursing*, 3(10):11-13, October, 1973.

Kubler-Ross, Elisabeth. "On death and dying". Therapeutic Grand Rounds, No. 36, *Journal of the American Medical Association*, 221(2):174-179, July 10, 1972.

Kubler-Ross, Elisabeth. "On the use of psychopharmacologic agents for the dying patient and the bereaved". *Journal of Thanatology*, 2:563-566, Winter-Spring, 1972.

Kubler-Ross, Elisabeth. "The right to die with dignity". *Bulletin of the Menninger Foundation*, 36(3):302-312, May, 1972.

Kubler-Ross, Elisabeth. "The stages of dying". PHP Institute of Tokyo, November, 1973.

Kubler-Ross, Elisabeth. "A teaching approach to the issues of death and dying". *Archives of the Foundation of Thanatology*, 2:125-127, Fall, 1970.

Kubler-Ross, Elisabeth. "What is it like to be dying?". *American Journal of Nursing*, 61(1):54-61, January, 1971.

Kuller, L. et. al. "Sudden and unexpected deaths in young adults. An epidemiological study". *Journal of American Medical Association,* 198:248-252, October, 1966.

Kutscher, Austin. "The foundation of thanatology". *Mental Hygiene,* 53:338-339, July, 1969.

Kyle, Sister M. Willa. "The nurse's approach to the patient attempting to adjust to inoperable cancer". *Nursing Research,* 14:178-179, Spring, 1965.

Lacasse, Christine Mitchell. "A dying adolescent". *American Journal of Nursing,* 75(3):433-434, March, 1975.

Laderman, Cecile. "On dying children: a mother speaks". *The National Observer,* May 17, 1975.

Lagemann, John Kord. "The hurt that heals". *Good Housekeeping,* 150:71, 176, 178-179, 182, 1960.

Lamers, Williams M., Jr. "Funerals are good for people - M.D.'s included". *Medical Economics,* 46:104-107, June 28, 1969.

Lamm, Maurice and Naftali Eskreis. "Viewing the remains: a new American custom". *Journal of Religion and Health,* 5(2):137-143, 1966.

Lancaster, H.O. "The mortality from violence in Australia, 1863 to 1960". *Medical Journal of Australia,* 1:388-393, 1964.

Lane, Margaret. "Disaster at sea". *Good Housekeeping,* 180(3):80+, March, 1975.

Lang, Priscilla A. and Jeannette R. Oppenheimer. "The influence of social work when parents are faced with the fatal illness of a child". *Social Casework,* 43(3):166, 1968.

Langsley, Donald G. "Psychology of a doomed family". *American Journal of Psychotherapy,* 15:531-538, 1961.

Lasker, Arnold A. "Telling children the facts of death". *Your Child,* 1-6, Winter, 1972.

Lascarl, A.D. "The family and the dying child: a compassionate approach". *Medical Times,* 97:207-215, May, 1969.

Lashal, L. and R.E. Worthington. "Some psychological correlates of neoplastic disease: a preliminary report". *Journal of Clinical and Experimental Psychopathology and the Quarterly Review of Psychiatric Neurology,* 16:281-288, 1955.

Lasker, Arnold A. "When children face bereavement". *Conservative Judaism,* 18:53-58, 1964.

Laws, E.H. et. al. "Views on euthanasia". *Journal of Medical Education*, 46:540, 1971.
Lazarus, Herbert and John J. Kosten, Jr. "Psychogenic hyperventilation and death anxiety". *Psychosomatics*, 10(1):14-22, 1969.
Leaf, Alexander. "Social consequences of new developments in medicine". *Bulletin of the Atomic Scientists*, 26(1):21-22, January, 1970.
Leddon, S.C. "Sleep paralysis, psychosis and death". *American Journal of Psychiatry*, 126:1027-1031, January, 1970.
Leeuwen, W.S. Van. "Symposium on the significance of EEG for 'statement on death'", Introduction. *Electroencephalography and Clinical Neurophysiology*, 27:214-215, August, 1969.
Lehrman, Samuel R. "Reactions to untimely death". *Psychiatric Quarterly*, 30:564-578, 1956.
Leng, G.A. "The problem of death". *Singapore Medical Journal*, 10:71, June, 1969.
LeShan, L. and E. LeShan. "Psychotherapy in the patient with a limited life span". *Psychiatry*, 24:4, November, 1961.
LeShan, L. and R.E. Worthington. "Some psychological correlates of neoplastic disease: a preliminary report". *Journal of Clinical and Experimental Psychopathology and the Quarterly Review of Psychiatric Neurology*, 16:281-288, 1955.
Lester, D. "The fear of the dead in non-literate societies". *Journal of Social Psychology*, 77:283-284, April, 1969.
Lester, D. "Studies on death-attitude scales". *Psychological Reports*, 24:180, February, 1969.
Lester, D. et. al. "Schizophrenia and death concern". *Journal of Projective Techniques and Personality Assessment*, 33:403-405, October, 1969.
Lester, David. "Antecedents of the fear of the dead". *Psychological Reports*, 19(3, Part 1):741-742, 1966.
Lester, David. "Checking on the harlequin". *Psychological Reports*, 19(3, Part 1):984+, 1966.
Lester, David. "Effects of suicide prevention centers on suicide in the U.S.". *Health Service Reports*, 89(1):37-39, January-February, 1974.
Lester, David. "Experimental and correlational studies of the fear of death". *Psychological Bulletin*, 67(1):27-36, 1967.

Letourneau, C.V. "A soliloquy on death". *Hospital Management,* 96:58-60, 1963.

"Let's talk about death". *Christopher News Notes,* No. 206: _____, May, 1974.

Leveton, Alan. "Time, death and ego-chill". *Journal of Existentialism,* 6(21):69-80, 1965.

Levin, A.J. "The fiction of the death instinct". *Psychiatric Quarterly,* 25:257, 1951.

Levin, Phyllis Lee. "Breaking the news of death". *The New York Times Magazine,* 47, February 21, 1965.

Leviton, D. "Crisis intervention by the health educator". *School Health Review,* 14-26, September, 1970.

Leviton, D. "Critical issues in health education. Editorial". *School Health Review,* November, 1969.

Leviton, Daniel, "Death, bereavement and suicide education", in Donald A. Read (ed.). *New Directions in Health Education,* New York: Macmillan Company, 1970.

Leviton, D. "Education for death; death education at the University of Maryland, College Park". *Journal of Health, Physical Education and Recreation,* 40:46-47, September, 1969.

Leviton, D. "A time to die". *Medical Journal of Australia,* 1:127-128, January, 1969.

Leviton, D. "Whether one lives or dies". *PHP International Magazine,* 4(11): November, 1973.

Leviton, Dan. "A course on death education and suicide prevention: implications for health education". *Journal of the American College Health Association,* 19(4):217-220, 1971.

Leviton, Dan. "Education for death, or death becomes less a stranger". *Omega: Journal of Death and Dying,* 6(3):183-193, 1975.

Leviton, Dan. "The need for education on death and suicide". *Journal of School Health,* 39:270-274, April, 1969.

Leviton, Dan. "The significance of sexuality as a deterrent to suicide among the aged". *Omega: Journal of Death and Dying,* 4(2):163+, Summer, 1973.

Levy, Norman B. "Fatal illness: should the patient be told?". *Medical Insight,* 20-23, November, 1973.

Lichtenwalner, Muriel E. "Children ask about death". *International Journal of Religious Education,* 40:14-16, June, 1964.

Lieberman, Morton A. "Observations on death and dying". *The Gerontologist*, 6:70-72, June, 1966.

Lieberman, Morton A. "Psychological correlates of impending death: some preliminary observations". *Journal of Gerontology*, 20:181-190, April, 1965.

Liegner, Leonard M. "St. Christopher's Hospice, 1974, care of the dying patient". *Journal of the American Medical Association*, 234(10):1047-1048, December 8, 1975.

"Life in death". Editorial. *New England Journal of Medicine*, 256(16):760-761, April 18, 1957.

"A life in the balance; case of K.A. Quinlan". *Time*, 106:52+, November 3, 1975.

Lifton, Robert J. "On death and death symbolism: the Hiroshima disaster". *Psychiatry*, 27:191-210, 1964.

Lifton, Robert J. "Psychological effects of the Atomic Bomb in Hiroshima: the theme of death". *Daedalus*, 92:462-497, 1963.

Lim, L.E. et. al. "Childhood mortality in the Philippines". *Journal of the Philippine Medical Association*, 41:304-312, 1965.

Lindeman, Bard. "Widower, heal thyself". *Today's Health*, 52(5):48-53, 1974.

Lindemann, Erich. "The meaning of crisis in individual and family". *Teachers College Record*, 57:310, 1956.

Lindemann, Erich. "Psychological aspects of mourning". *The Director*, 31:14-17, 1961.

Lindemann, Erich. "Symptomology and management of acute grief". *American Journal of Psychiatry*, 101:141-148, 1944.

Lindemann, Erich and Ina May Greer. "A study of grief: emotional responses to suicide". *Pastoral Psychology*, 4:9-13, 1953.

Linkletter, Art. "What I've learned about drugs since my daughter's death". *Good Housekeeping*, 181:89+, November, 1975.

Lipson, Channing T. "Denial and mourning". *International Journal of Psychoanalysis*, 44:104-107, 1963.

Lirette, W.L. "Management of patients with terminal cancer". *Postgraduate Medicine*, 46:145-149, December, 1969.

Liston, Edward. "Education on death and dying: a survey of American medical schools". *Journal of Medical Education*, 48:577-578, 1973.

Litman, R.E. "Psychological-psychiatric aspects in certifying modes of death". *Journal of Forensic Science*, 13:46-54, January, 1968.

Litman, Robert. "Doctors killing themselves". *Science Digest*, 76(4):49, October, 1974.

Litman, Robert E. "When patients commit suicide". *American Journal of Psychotherapy*, 19:570-576, October, 1965.

"Little murderers" *Time*, 100:102, October 23, 1972.

Loesser, Lewis H. and Thea Bry. "The role of death fears in the etiology of phobic anxiety as reversal in group psychotherapy". *International Journal of Group Psychotherapy*, 10:287-297, 1960.

Logsdon, Gene. "Will she ever live again?". *Farm Journal*, 94:44-45+, April, 1976.

"Longevity: ah, to be young while old . . .". *Harpers*, 246(1477):3-11, June, 1973.

Lopata, Helena Z. "Living through widowhood". *Psychology Today*, 7(2):87-92, 1973.

Lourie, R S. "The pediatrician and the handling of terminal illness". *Pediatrics*, 32:477-479, 1963.

Love, Ann B. "Surviving widowhood". *Ms. Magazine*, 111(4):84-91, October, 1974.

Lovette, Roger. "Grief - and you and me". *Pulpit Digest*, 44, January, 1972.

Lucente, Frank. 'Thanatology, a study of 100 deaths on an otolarngology service". *Omega: Journal of Death and Dying*, 3:211-216, 1972.

Luke, J.L. "Certification of death by coroner". *New England Journal of Medicine*, 280:1364, June 12, 1969.

Luke, J.L et. al., "Sudden unexpected death from natural causes in young adults. A review of 275 consecutive autopsied cases". *Archives of Pathology*, 85:10-17, January, 1968.

Lund, D.H. "Helping children cope with sorrow". *Parent's Magazine*, 50(2):42-43+, February, 1975.

Luria, S.M. "Average age at death of scientists in various specialities". *Public Health Report*, 84:661-664, 1969.

MacCarthy, D. "The repercussions of the death of a child". *Proceedings of the Royal Society of Medicine*, 62:553-554, June, 1969.

McClure, John. "Death education". *Phi Delta Kappan*, 55:483-485, 1974.

McGann, Leona M. "The cancer patient's needs: how can we meet them?". *Journal of Rehabilitation*, 30(6):19, 1964.
McCleave, Paul B. "Medicine seeks the clergy". *Journal of Religion and Health*, 2:239-247, April, 1963.
McCollum, Audrey T. and A. Herbert Schwartz. "Social work and the mourning parent". *Social Work*, 17(1):25-36, 1972.
McConville, B.J. et. al. "Mourning depressive responses of children in residence following sudden death of a parent". *Journal of the American Academy of Child Psychiatry*, 11:341-364, 1972.
McCormick, Richard. "The preservation of life". *Linacre Quarterly*, 43(2):94-100, 1976.
McCormick, Richard A. "To save or let die". *America*, 13:6-10, July 13, 1974.
McCorry, V.P. "Face the fact: Holy Week bids us face the fact of life which is death". *America*, 120:372-373, March 29, 1969.
McCully, Robert S. "Fantasy productions of children with a progressively crippling and fatal illness". *The Journal of Genetic Psychology*, 102:203-216, 1963.
McDonald, Arthur. "Death psychology of historical personages". *American Journal of Psychology*, 33:552-556, 1921.
McDonald, M. "Farewell to a friend". *American Journal of Nursing*, 68:773, April, 1968.
McDonald, Morris J. "The management of grief: a study of black funeral practices". *Omega: Journal of Death and Dying*, 4(2):139+, Spring, 1973.
McGee, R.K. "The suicide prevention center or a model for community mental health programs". *Community Mental Health Journal*, 1(2):162-170, 1965.
McIntire, Matilda A. and Carol R. Angle. "The concept of death in Midwestern children and youth". *American Journal of Diseases of Children*, 123(6):527-532, June, 1972.
McMahan, J.D. "Death education: an independent study unit". *Journal of School Health*, 43:526-527, 1973.
McMahon, Joan D. "A unit for independent study in death education". *School Health Review*, 4(4):27-43, 1973.
McManus, F.R. "The reformed funeral rite". *American Ecclesiastical Review*, 166:45-59, 124-139, January-February, 1972.
McVay, Linda. "An interaction study involving a patient with a guarded prognosis". *American Journal of Nursing*, 66:1071-1073, June, 1966.

Madden, Julie. "An analysis of the euphemisms of death and dying". *The Director*, 8+, January, 1966.

Madden, Maureen. "Let's try to face death instead of fearing it". *Seventeen*, 34:40, July, 1975.

Maddison, D. "The nurse and the dying patient". *Nursing Times*, 65:265-266, February, 1969.

Maddison, D. "The relevance of conjugal bereavement for preventive psychiatry". *British Journal of Medical Psychology*, 41:223-233, September, 1968.

Maddison, D. and A. Viola. "The health of widows in the year following bereavement". *Journal of Psychosomatic Research*, 12:297, 1968.

Maddison, D.C. and W.L. Walker. "Factors affecting the outcome of conjugal bereavement". *British Journal of Psychiatry*, 113:1057, 1967.

Maddison, D.C., A. Viola and W. Walker. "Further studies in conjugal bereavement". *Australian and New Zealand Journal of Psychiatry*, 3:63, 1969.

Madow, L. and S.E. Hardy. "Incidence and analysis of the broken family in the background of neurosis". *American Journal of Orthopsychiatry*, 17:521-528, 1947.

Malloy, Paul. "Death with dignity". *U.S. Catholic*, 7-11, February, 1975.

Maguire, Daniel C. "Death by chance, death by choice". *The Atlantic Monthly*, 233(1):57-65, 1974.

Maguire, Daniel C. "Death, legal and illegal". *Atlantic Monthly*, 233(2):72-85, February, 1974.

Mahler, Margaret S. "Helping children to accept death". *Child Study*, 27:98-99, 1950.

Maisel, A.Q. "Facts you should know about funerals". *Reader's Digest*, 89:81-86, September, 1966.

Malino, Jerome R. "Coping with death in western religious civilization". *Zygon - Journal of Religion and Science*, 1(4):354-365, December, 1966.

Malinowski, Bronisaw. "Baloma: the spirits of the dead in the Trobriand Islands". *Journal of the Royal Anthropological Institute of Great Britain and Ireland*, 46:353-430, 1916.

Mason, J.K. et. al. "Multiple disinterments in equatorial Africa". *Aerospace Medicine*, 36:636-639, 1965.

Manabe, H. et. al. "Determination of death of the heart donor". *Naika*, 23:854-860, May, 1969.

Mandel, Nathan G. "Treatment of the aged mentally ill". *Geriatrics*, 15:407-412, May, 1960.

Mannes, Marya. "Euthanasia vs. the right to life". *The Student Lawyer*, 3(5):18-19+, January, 1975.

Marcovitz, Eli. "What is the meaning of death to the dying person and his survivors?". *Omega: Journal of Death and Dying*, 4(1):13-25, 1973.

Marriott-Watson, H.B. "Some thoughts on pain and death". *North American Review*, 173:540, 1961.

Marshall, Joanne Gard. "Annotated bibliography: a selected list of children's books relating to death". *Omega: Journal of Death and Dying*, 2:41-45, 1971.

Marshall, Victor W. "The treatment of death in children's books". *Omega: Journal of Death and Dying*, 2:36-41, 1971.

Marthinson, Ida. "Why don't we let them die at home?". *R.N.*, 39(1):58-65, January, 1976.

Martin, D. and L. Wrightsman. "Religion and fears about death; a critical review of research". *Religious Education*, 59:174-176, 1964.

Martin, D. et. al. "The relationship between religious behavior and concern about death". *Journal of Social Psychology*, 65:317-323, April, 1965.

Martin, Mildred Crowl. "Helping children cope with sorrow". *Parent's Magazine*, 45:42-43, August, 1976.

Martin, Phyllis. "My problem - widow!". *Good Housekeeping*, 182(3):18+, 1976.

Mastin, B.A. "The extend burials at the Mugharet Elwad". *Journal of the Royal Anthropological Institute of Great Britain and Ireland*, 94(1):44-51, January-June, 1964.

Mathis, James L. "A sophisticated version of voodoo death". *Psychosomatic Medicine*, 26:104, 1964.

"Matter of death and life: life-giving death". *Christian Century*, 81:291, March 4, 1964.

Mattison, Margaret. "Love is not enough". *Reader's Digest*, 108(646):79-82, February, 1976.

Matz, Milton. "Judaism and bereavement". *Journal of Religion and Health*, 3:345-352, 1964.

Maurer, Adah. "Adolescent attitudes toward death". *Journal of Genetics and Psychology*, 105:75-90, 1964.

Maurer, Adah. "The child's knowledge of nonexistence". *Journal of Existential Psychiatry*, 2:193-212, 1961.

Maurer, Adah. "The game of peek-a-boo". *Diseases of the Nervous System*, 28(2):118-121, 1967.

Maurer, Adah. "Maturation of concepts of death". *British Journal of Medicine and Psychology*, 39:35-41, 1966.

Maxwell, I. "When to turn off the respirator". *Nova Scotia Medical Bulletin*, 47:225-226, December, 1968.

Means, Marie Hackl. "Fears of one thousand college women". *Journal of Abnormal and Social Psychology*, 31:348-363, 1936.

Medici, Frank N. "Battling mysterious crib death". *Reader's Digest*, 102(613):137-140, May, 1973.

Melear, John D. "Children's conceptions of death". *Journal of Genetic Psychology*, 123(2):359-360, 1973.

Meerloo, Joost. "Psychological implications of malignant growth: a survey of hypothesis". *British Journal of Medical Psychology*, 27:210-215, 1954.

Meisel, A.M. et. al. "Reactions to approaching death". *Diseases of the Nervous System*, 26:15-24, January, 1965.

Meissner, W.W. "Affective response to psychoanalytic death symbols". *Journal of Abnormal and Social Psychology*, 56:295-299, 1958.

Mendaldino, R, "The cemeteries of Turin from the hygienico-sanitary point of view". *Minerva Medica*, 56:907-909, 1965.

Menninger, E. "Death from psychic causes". *Bulletin of the Menninger Clinic*, 12:31-36, 1948.

Menninger, Karl. "Dr. Karl's reading notes". *Menninger Library Journal*, 1:15, 1956.

Menzies, Isabel E. "Thoughts on the maternal role in contemporary society". *Journal of Child Psychotherapy*, 4:5-14, 1975.

Menzies, Isabel E.P. "A case study in the functioning of social systems as a defense against anxiety: a report of a study of the nursing service of a general hospital". *Human Relations*, 13:95-121, May, 1960.

Merrill, J.P. "Clinical experience is tempered by genuine human concern". *Journal of the American Medical Association*, 189:626-627, 1964.

Merrill, J.P. "Statement of the Committee on Morals and Ethics of the Transplantation Society". *Annals of Internal Medicine*, 75:631-633, 1971.

Meyers, David W. "The legal aspects of medical euthanasia". *Bioscience*, 23(8):467, August, 1973.

Meyers, Mary Ema. "Nursing the comatose patient". *American Journal of Nursing*, 54:716-718, June, 1954.

Meyerson, Abraham. "Prolonged cases of grief reactions treated by electric shock". *New England Journal of Medicine*, 230:255-256, 1944.

Michaelson, Mike. "For now I'll go on being Father and Mother". *Today's Health*, 50:52-57, 1972.

Michaelson, Mike. "The love that lights the last days of a brave young mother". *Today's Health*, 49:49-53, 62-65, 1971.

Middleton, Carl. "Principles of life-death decision-making". *Linacre Quarterly*, 42(4):268-277, 1975.

Middleton, W.C. "Some reactions toward death among college students". *Journal of Abnormal and Social Psychology*, 31:165-173, 1936.

Miles, Helen and Dorothea R. Hays. "Widowhood". *American Journal of Nursing*, 75(2):280-282, February, 1975.

Miller, C.R., G. Sabagh and H.F. Dingman. "Latent class analysis and differential mortality". *Journal of the American Statistical Association*, 57:403-438, June, 1962.

Miller, Catherin M. "Crisis intervention and health counseling". *School Health Review*, 1(3):15-17, 1970.

Miller, Jill. "Children's reactions to the death of a parent: a review of the psychoanalytic literature". *American Psychoanalytic Association Journal*, 19:697-719, 1971.

Miller, Peter G. and Jan Ozga. "Mommy, what happens when I die?". *Mental Hygiene*, 57:20-22, Spring, 1973.

Miller, R.W. "Childhood cancer and congenital defects. A study of U.S. death certificates during the period 1960-1966". *Pediatric Research*, 3:389-397, September, 1969.

Mills, D.H. "Medicolegal ramifications of current practices and suggested changes in certifying modes of death". *Journal of Forensic Science*, 13:70-75, January, 1968.

Mira Y Lopez, E. "Psychopathology of anger and fear reactions in wartime". *American Clinician*, 5:98-106, 1943.

Mise, J. et. al. "Management of life prolongation at the terminal stage and its discontinuation". *Naika*, 23:839-844, May, 1969.
Mitchell, Nelli E. "The significance of the loss of the father through death". *American Journal of Orthopsychiatry*, 34:279-280, 1964.
Mitford, Jessica. "Have the undertakers reformed". *Atlantic*, 215:69-73, June, 1965.
Mitra, D.N. "Mourning customs and modern life in Bengal". *American Journal of Sociology*, 52:309-311, 1947.
Miyahara, M. "Determination of death in heart transplantation". *Naika*, 23:850-853, May, 1969.
Moellenhoff, F. "Ideas of children about death". *Bulletin of the Menninger Clinic*, 3:148-156, 1939.
Moellenhoff, Fritz. "Ideas of children about death". *Bulletin of the Menninger Clinic*, 3:148-156, 1939.
"The moment of death". *South African Medical Journal*,43:50, January 18, 1969.
Monro, Alistair. "Childhood parent loss in a psychiatrically normal population". *British Journal of Preventive Social Medicine*, 19:69-70, 1965.
Monsour, Karen J. "Asthma and the fear of death". *Psychoanalytic Quarterly*, 29:56-71, 1960.
Monteiro, Louis. "Disengagement in the chronically ill; an application of sociological theory to nursing observations". *Nursing Research*, 14:175, Spring, 1965.
Moor, P. "Speaking out: let the dying die". *Saturday Evening Post*, 239:12+, September 10, 1966.
Moore, Donald J. "The final and grandest act". *America*, 133(8): 165-168, September 27, 1975.
Moore, F.D. "Ethics in the new medicine - tissue transplants". *The Nation*, 200(14):358-362, April 5, 1965.
Moore, Gerald. "A year in the shadow of death". *Reader's Digest*, 108(650):66-70, June, 1976.
Moore, Honor. "What it feels like to be dying". *MS*, 4:15-22, May, 1976.
Moore, Joan. "The death culture of Mexico and Mexican-Americans". *Omega: Journal of Death and Dying*, 1:271-291, 1970.

Moore, Wilbert E. "Time - the ultimate scarcity". *The American Behavioral Scientist*, 6:58-60, May, 1963.

Moran, P.A. "Maternal age and parental loss". *British Journal of Psychiatry*, 114:207-214, February, 1968.

Moran, P.A. and K. Abe. "Parental loss in homosexuals". *British Journal of Psychiatry*, 115:319-320, 1969.

"Moratorium day". *American Journal of Nursing*, 69:2645, December, 1969.

More, Thomas. "Euthanasia in utopia". *Child and Family*, 11(1):86-87, 1972.

Moreno, J.L. "The social atom and death". *Sociometry*, 10:80-84, 1947.

Morgenthau, Hans J. "Death in the nuclear age". *Commentary*, 32:231, 1961.

Moriarty, D.M. "Early loss and the fear of mothering". *Psychoanalysis and the Psychoanalytic Review*, 49:63-69, 1962.

Morison, R.S. "Death: process or event?". *Science*, 173:694-698, 1972.

Moritz, Alan R. "Sudden deaths". *New England Journal of Medicine*, 223(20):798-801, November 14, 1940.

Moritz, Alan R. and Norman Zamcheck. "Sudden and unexpected death of young soldiers". *Archives of Pathology*, 42:459-494, 1946.

Moriyama, I.M. "The change in mortality trend in the United States". *Vital Health Statistics*, 3:1-43, 1964.

Morrison, Robert S. "Dying" *Scientific American*, 229(3):54-62, 1973.

Morrissey, James R. "Children's adaptation to fatal illness". *Social Work*, 8:81-88, 1963.

Morrissey, James R. "Death anxiety in children with a fatal illness". *American Journal of Psychotherapy*, 18:606-615, 1964.

Morrissey, James R. "A note on interviews with children facing imminent death". *Social Casework*, 44:343-345, 1963.

"Mortality trends in the western world". *Geriatrics*, 24:64, 1969.

Moses, Lincoln E. and Frederick Mosteller. "Institutional differences in post-operative death rates". *The Journal of the American Medical Association*, 203(7):492-494, February 12, 1968.

"A move to embalm, 'cremation clubs' ". *Business Week*, No. 2349:89, September 21, 1974.

Muggeridge, M. "Christmas diary". *New Statesman*, 78:920, December, 1969.
Muhsam, H.V. "Differential mortality in Israel by socio-economic status". *Eugenics Quarterly*, 12:227-232, December, 1965.
Munro, A. et. al. "Further data on childhood parent-loss in psychiatric normals, *Acta Physiologica Scandinavica*, 44:485-500, 1968.
Murgoci, A. "Customs connected with death and burial among the Roumanians". *Folklore*, 30:89-102, 1919.
Murphy, Robert. "A Christian funeral director's reflections on the modern funeral". *Linacre Quarterly*, 42(4):279-285, 1975.
Muslim, Hyman L., Susan P., and Harold Levine. "Partners in dying". *American Journal of Psychiatry*, 131(3):308-314, 1974.
Nagy, Maria H. "The child's theories concerning death". *Journal of Genetic Psychology*, 73:3-27, 1948.
Nagy, Maria H. "The child's view of death". *Journal of Genetics and Psychology*, 73:3-27, 1948.
Nahum, Louis H. "Dealing with the last chapter of life". *Connecticut Medicine*, 30:170-174, March, 1966.
Nahum, Louis H. "The dying patient's grief". *Connecticut Medicine*, 28:241-245, April, 1964.
Nakagawa, Y. "Standards for determining death. Philosophy of death under present standards of medical practice". *Surgical Therapy*, 20:405-408, April, 1969.
Natason, Maurice. "Death and situation". *American Imago*, 4:35-42, 1959.
Nathan, H. et. al. "Death and the physician in art". *Medizinische Welt*, 52:2845-2852, December 28, 1968.
Natterson, J.M. and A.G. Knudson. "Observations concerning fear of death in fatally il children and their mothers". *Psychosomatic Medicine* 22:456-466, 1960.
Neale, A.V. "The changing pattern of death in childhood: then and now". *Medical Science Law*, 4:35-39, 1964.
Needleman, Jacob. "Imagining absence, non-existence and death: a sketch". *Review of Existential Psychology and Psychiatry*, 6(3):230-236, 1966.
Neuring, C. "Divergencies between attitudes towards life and death among suicidal, psychosomatic, and normal hospitalized patients". *Journal of Consulting Clinical Psychology*, 32:59-63, February, 1968.

Nemtzow, Jesse and Stanley R. Lesser. "Reactions of children and parents to the death of President Kennedy". *American Journal of Orthopsychiatry*, 34:280-281, 1964.

Nevin, D. "Home to Abilene". *Life*, 66:24-35, April 11, 1969.

"A new ethic for medicine and society". *California Medicine*, 113:67-68, 1970.

"New venture". *Reader's Digest*, 55:125-126, July, 1949.

Nix, J.T. "Study of the relationship of environmental factors to the type and frequency of cancer causing death in Nuns". *Hospital Progress*, 45:71-74, 1964.

Niyogi, A.K. et. al. Diurnal variations in death". *Indian Journal of Medical Research*, 52:1092-1098, 1964.

Nobbe, George. "How science hopes to cheat death". *New York Sunday News*, 74-75, January 29, 1967.

Nolfi, W.W. "Families in grief: the question of casework intervention". *Social Casework*, 12(3):40-6, 1967.

Noon, John A. " A preliminary examination of the death concepts of the Ibo". *American Anthropologist*, 44:638-654, 1942.

Noonan, Lynn P. "Five seasons of sadness". *Journal of Psychiatric Nursing and Mental Health Services*, 13:22-28, 1975.

Noonan, Lynn and Judy Tiktinsky. "The dying child and his family: a unique approach". *American Journal of Orthopsychiatry*, 45:257-258, 1975.

Norris, Catherine M. "The nurse and the dying patient". *American Journal of Nursing*, 55:1214-1217, October, 1955.

Northrup, Fran C. "The dying child". *American Journal of Nursing*, 74(6):1066-1068, 1974.

Norton, J. "Treatment of a dying female patient". *Psyche*, 22:99-107, February, 1968.

"Notes of a dying professor". *Nursing Outlook*, 20(8):502-506, 1972.

Noyes, Russell, Jr. "Suicide: motivation and prevention". *Postgraduate Medicine*, 47(3):182-187, March, 1970.

O'Connell, Walter. "The humor of the gallows". *Omega: Journal of Death and Dying*, 1(4):31-33, December, 1966.

O'Donnel, Thomas J. "To live - to die". *Journal of the American Medical Association*, 228:501, April 22, 1974.

Oelrich, Margaret. "The patient with a fatal illness". *American Journal of Occupational Therapy*, 28(7):429-434, 1974.

O'Hare, Joseph. "Karen Anne Quinlan and the right to die". *America*, 134:327-328, April 17, 1976.

Okinaka, S. "Internist's view of the terminal state". *Naika*, 23:804-807, May, 1969.

Olin, Harry. "A proposed model to teach medical students the care of the dying patient". *Journal of Medical Education*, 47:564-576, 1972.

Oman, John B. "Community responsibility to the grieving". *The Dodge Magazine*, 67(3):20-21, 29+, June, 1975.

Oman, John B. "How the family deals with the bereaved". *The Dodge Magazine*, 67(4):20, September, 1975.

Oman, John B. "The many faces of death". *The Dodge Magazine*, 67(2):12, March, 1975.

Oman, John B. "The widow/widower". *The Dodge Magazine*, 67(1): _____ , January, 1975.

Opler, Morris E. and William E. Bittle. "The death practices and eschatology of the Kiowa Apache". *Southwestern Journal of Anthropology*, 17:383-394, 1961.

Oppenheimer, Jeannette R. "Use of crisis intervention in casework with the cancer patient and his family". *Social Casework*, 12(2):44-52, 1967.

Orbach, Charles E. "The multiple meanings of the loss of a child". *American Journal of Psychotherapy*, 13:906-915, 1959.

Orbach, Charles E., Arthur M. Sutherland and Mary F. Bozeman. "Psychological impact of cancer and its treatment: III. The adaptation of mothers to the threatened loss of their children through leukemia: Part 1". *Cancer*, 8:1-19, 1955.

Orbach, Charles E., Arthur M. Sutherland, and Mary F. Bozeman. "Psychological impact of cancer and its treatment: III. The adaptation of mothers to the threatened loss of their children through leukemia: Part II". *Cancer*, 8:20-33, 1955.

Orlansky, Harold. "Reactions to the death of President Roosevelt". *Journal of Social Psychology*, 26:235-266, 1947.

Ostrow, Mortimer. "The death instincts: a contribution to the study of instincts". *International Journal of Psychoanalysis*, 39(Part 1):5-16, 1958.

"Out of darkness: preparing the dying for the inevitable". *Time*, 94:60, October 10, 1969.

Page, I.H. "The ethics of heart transplantation". *Journal of the American Medical Association*, 207:109-113, 1969.

Page, I.H. "Prolongation of life in affluent society". *Review of Modern Medicine*, 20-21, 1963.

Pahnke, W.N. "Psychedelic mystical experiences in human encounter with death". *Harvard Theological Review*, 62:1-32, January, 1969. (with replies by H.K. Beecher and G.D. Kaufman).

Palmer, Lane. "Conversations with a dying son". *Farm Journal*, 100(3): 38-39+, Mid-February, 1976.

Paris, J. et. al. "Responses to death and sex stimulus materials as a function of repression-sensitization". *Psychological Reports*, 19:1283-1291, December, 1966.

Parkes, C.M. "Bereavement and mental illness. Pt. I, A clinical study of the grief of bereaved psychiatric patients. Pt. 2, A classification of bereavement reactions". *British Journal of Medical Psychology*, 38:1, 1965.

Parkes, C.M. "Broken heart; a statistical study of increased mortality among widowers". *British Medical Journal*, 1:740-743, 1969.

Parkes, C.M. "The first year of bereavement: a longitudinal study of the reaction of London widows to the death of their husbands". *Psychiatry*, 33:444, 1971.

Parkes, C.M. "Recent bereavement as a cause of mental illness". *British Journal of Psychiatry*, 110:198, 1964a.

Parkes, C. Murray. "Bereavement and mental illness: Part I. Clinical study of grief of bereaved psychiatric patients; Part II. A classification of bereavement reactions". *British Journal of Medical Psychology*, 38:1-26, March 1965.

Parkes, C. Murray. "Effects of bereavement on physical and mental health--a study of the medical records on widows". *British Medical Journal*, 2:274-279, 1964.

Parkes, C. Murray. "Grief as an illness". *New Society*, 9:11-12, April 9, 1964.

Parkes, C. Murray. "Recent bereavement as a cause of mental illness". *British Journal of Psychiatry*, 110:198-203, 1964.

Parkes, C. Murray and R.J. Brown. "Health after bereavement: a controlled study of young Boston widows and widowers". *Psychosomatic Medicine*, 34(5):449-461, 1972.

Parkes, Colin Murray. "Components of the reaction to loss of limb, spouse, or home". *Journal of Psychosomatic Research*, 16:343-349, 1972.

Parkes, Colin Murray. "Determination of outcome of bereavement". *Proceedings of the Royal Society of Medicine*, 64:279, 1971.

Parkin, Michael. "A proposal for the development of crisis counseling services related to dying, death, grief and mourning". *Crisis Intervention*, 4(4):121-125, 1972.

Parsons, Talcott. "Death in American society - a brief working paper". *The American Behavioral Scientist*, 6:61-65, 1963.

Patry, F.L. "A psychiatric evaluation of communicating with the dying". *Diseases of the Nervous System*, 27:715-718, November, 1965.

Pattison, E.M. "Psychosocial predictors of death prognosis". *Omega: Journal of Death and Dying*, 5(2):145-160, 1974.

Pattison, E. Mansell. "The experience of dying". *American Journal of Psychology*, 21(1):23-43, 1967.

Patton, Kenneth. "Science, religion and death". *Zygon - Journal of Religion and Science*, 1(4):332-346, December, 1966.

Paul, Norman L. "Empathic escavation of buried grief". *Roche Report: Frontiers of Clinical Psychiatry*, 4:1-2+, February 15, 1967.

Paul, Norman L. and G.H. Gorsser. "Operational mourning and its role in conjoint family therapy". *Community Mental Health Journal*, 1:339-345, 1965.

Pearlman, Joel, Bernard A. Stotsky and Juan R. Dominick. "Attitudes toward death among nursing home personnel". *Journal of Genetic Psychology*, 114:63-75, 1969.

Paz, Octavio. "The eye of Mexico: Todos Santos, Dia de Muertos". *Evergreen Review*, 2:22-37, 1959.

Pearson, L.S. "Medical certification of death". *Pennsylvania Medicine*, 72:17, March 1969.

Peck, M. "Notes on identification in a case of depression reactive to the death of a love object". *Psychoanalytic Quarterly*, 8:1-17, 1939.

Peniston, D.H. "The importance of death education in family life". *Family Life Coordinator*, 11:15-18, 1962.

Pentney, B.H. "Grief". *Nursing Times*, 60:1496-1498, November 13, 1964.

Pericoli, Ridolfini F. "The diagnosis of death". *Policlinco Sezione Practica*, 76:865-877, July 7, 1969.

Perske, Robert. "Death and ministry: episode and response". *Pastoral Psychology*, 15:25-35, 1964.

Peterson, William D., Sartore, Richard L. "Helping Children Cope With Death," *Elementary School Guidance and Counseling* 226-232, March, 1975.

"The phantom limb". *Transaction*, 4:5, July-August, 1967.

Phipps, Joyce. "What really happens when your husband dies". *Christian Century*, 90(8):230-232, February 21, 1973.

Pike, Diane Kennedy. "Bishop Pike's messages from beyond the grave". *Ladies Home Journal*, 87(11):87+, November, 1970.

Pilsecker, Carleton. "Help for the dying". *Social Work*, 20(3):190-4, May, 1975.

Pincherle, G. "Mortality of members of Parliament". *British Journal of Preventive Sociological Medicine*, 23:72-76, 1969.

Pine, Vanderlyn R. "Comparative funeral practices". *Practical Anthropology*, 16:49-62, March-April, 1969.

Pine, Vanderlyn R. "Institutionalized communication about dying and death". *Journal of Thanatology*, 3(1):1-12, 1975.

Pine, Vanderlyn R. "The role of the funeral director in disaster". *The Director*, 39:11-13, August, 1969.

Pine, Vanderlyn R. "Social organization and death". *Omega: Journal of Death and Dying*, 149-153, February, 1972.

Pine, Vanderlyn R. and Derek Phillips. "The cost of dying: a sociological analysis of funeral expenditure". *Social Problems*, 17:415-417, Winter, 1970.

"Pitfalls to watch for in planning your estate". *U.S. News and World Report*, 73(25):48-57, December 18, 1972.

Platt, R. "Reflections on aging and death". *Lancet*, 1:1-6, June 5, 1963.

Pohl, Frederick. "Intimations of immortality". *Playboy Magazine*, 11(6):79-80, June, 1964.

Pokorny, A.D. "Moon phases, suicide and homicide". *American Journal of Psychiatry*, 121:66-67, July, 1964.

Pollack, Jack. "I want out". *Today's Health*, 49:32-34, 1971.

Pollock, G.H. "Mourning and adaptation". *International Journal of Psychoanalysis*, 42:341-361, 1961.

Pollock, G.S. "Childhood parent and sibling loss in adult patients". *Archives of Genetic Psychiatry* 7:295-306, 1962.

Pomeroy, Margaret R. "Sudden death syndrome". *American Journal of Nursing*, 69(9):1886-1890, September, 1969.
Pompey, H. "Brain death and total death. Moral and theological aspects of heart transplants". *Munchener Medizinische Wochenschrift*, 111:736-741, March 28, 1969.
Potthoff, C.J. "First aid: determination of death". *Today's Health*, 47:74, September, 1969.
Pound, Louise. "American euphemisms for dying, death and burial". *American Speech*, 11:195-202, 1936.
Pressey, S.L. "Age counseling: crises, services, potentials". *Journal of Counseling Psychology*. 20(4):356-360, 1973.
Pressey, Sidney L. "Crises, services, potentials". *Journal of Counseling Psychology*, 20(4):356-360, 1973.
Pretty, L.C. "Ministering to the bereaved and dying". *Nebraska State Medical Journal*, 44:243-249, 1959.
Pretzel, P. "The volunteer clinical worker at the S.P.C.". *Bulletin of Suicidology*, no. 6:29-34, Spring, 1970.
Price, E.D. "The 'view' with implications". *Medico-legal Journal*, 32-92-94, 1964.
"Profile of the organ donor". *Psychology Today*, 9(7):28+, 1975.
"Progress in organ transplants". *U.S. News and World Report*, 78(4):40, January 27, 1975.
"Protocol for the determination of death endorsed by the Allegheny County Ad Hoc Committee on Tissue Transplantation". *Pennsylvania Medicine*, 72:17-20, March, 1969.
Purci-Jones, John et. al. "Temporal stability and change in attitudes toward the Kennedy assassination". *Psychological Reports*, 23(3):907-913, 1969.
Puffer, R.R. et. al. "Cooperative international research on mortality". *Boletin de la Ofician Sanitaria Panamericana*, 58:1-16, 1965.
Puffer, R.R. et. al. "International collaborative research on mortality". *World Health Organization, Public Health Papers*, 27:113-130, 1965.
"Pulling the plug . . . is it murder or mercy?". *Ladies Home Journal*, 93(3):98-99, March, 1976.
Purpura, G. "Civilizations practicing interment and cremation". *Annali della Sanita Publica*, 27:188-197, January-February, 1966.

Quevauviller, A. "The public health specialist in the face of death". *Products et Problems Pharmaceutiques*, 19:505-518, 1964.

Quint, Jeanne C. "Awareness of death and the nurse's composure". *Nursing Research*, 15:49-55, Winter, 1966.

Quint, Jeanne C. "The dying patient: a difficult nursing problem". *Nursing Clinics of North America*, 2:763+, December, 1967.

Quint, Jeanne C. "Hidden hazards for nurse teachers". *Nursing Outlook*, 15:34-35, April, 1967.

Quint, Jeanne C. "Institutionalized practices of information control". *Psychiatry: Journal for the Study of Interpersonal Processes*, 28:119-132, May, 1965.

Quint, Jeanne C. "Mastectomy: signpost in time". *The Journal of Nursing Education*, 2:3-11, September, 1963.

Quint, Jeanne C. "Mastectomy - symbol of cure or warning sign?". *American Academy of General Practice*, 29:119-124, 1964.

Quint, Jeanne C. "Nursing services and the care of dying patients: some speculations". *Nursing Science*, 2:432-443, December, 1964.

Quint, Jeanne C. "Obstacles to helping the dying". *American Journal of Nursing*, 66:1568-1571, July, 1966.

Quint, Jeanne C. "The threat of death: some consequences for patients and nurses". *Nursing Forum*, 8(3):2864, 1969.

Quint, Jeanne C. and Anselm L. Strauss. "Nursing students assignments and dying patients". *Nursing Outlook* 12:24-27, 1964.

Radford, John, "An image of death in dreams and ballads". *International Journal of Symbology*, 6(3):15-22, November, 1975.

Rado, Sandor. "The problem of melancholia". *International Journal of Psychoanalysis*, 9:420-438, 1928.

Rahe, R., J. McKean and R.J. Arthur. "A longitudinal study of life-change and illness patterns". *Journal of Psychosomatic Research*,10:365, 1967.

Rahe, R., M. Meyer, et al. "Social stress and illness onset". *Journal of Psychosomatic Research*, 8:35-43, 1964.

Rakoff, V.M. "Psychiatric aspects of death in America". *Social Research*, 39:515-527, 1972.

Ramos, Suzanne. "Learning about death: the hardest lesson of all". *New York Times Magazine*, 94-95+, December 10, 1972.

Rapaport, Henry N. "Funeral practices - U.S. model 1965". *The Torch*, 28-32, Spring, 1965.

Ravensborg, M.R. et. al. "Suicide and natural death in a state hospital population: a comparison of admission complaints, MMPI profiles and social competence factors". *Journal of Consulting Clinical Psychology*, 33:466-471, August, 1969.

Ray, S.K. et. al. "Exhumation". *Journal of Indian Medical Association*, 46:193-197, February, 1966.

"Recent mortality trends in the Western world". *Statistical Bulletin*, Metropolitan Life Insurance Co., 46:1-4, August, 1965.

Regan, P.T. "The dying patient and his family". *Journal of the American Medical Association*, 192:666-667, 1965.

Reid, D.D. et. al. "Assessing the comparability of mortality statistics". *British Medical Journal*, 5422:1437-1439, 1964.

Reid, Fred W., Jr. "Prolongation of life or prolongation of the act of dying". *Journal of the American Medical Association*, 201(2):162-163, October 9, 1967.

Reilly, C.T. "The diagnosis of life and death". *Journal of the Medical Society of New Jersey*, 66:601-604, November, 1969.

Rees, W.D. and Sylvia Lutkins. "Mortality of bereavement". *British Medical Journal*, 4:13-16, 1967.

Remsberg, B. and C. Remsberg. "What four brave women told their children". *Good Housekeeping*, 164:94-96, May, 1967.

Remsberg, Bonnie. "My mother wouldn't let me die". *Good Housekeeping*, 182(6):97+, June, 1976.

Remsberg, Bonnie and Charles. "Second thoughts on abortion from the doctor who led the crusade for it". *Good Housekeeping*, 182(3):69+, 1976.

Renshaw, Charles C., Jr. "The changing dimensions of death". *Prism*, 3(6):17, June, 1975.

Renshaw, Domeena C. "Suicide and depression in children". *The Journal of School Health*, 44(9):487-489, 1974.

"A report from heaven". *Newsweek*, 79(1):52, January 3, 1972.

Reynolds, B.R. "Eerie need to redefine death". *America*, 133:162-174, September, 27, 1975.

Reynolds, David K. and Richard A. Kalish. "Work roles in death related occupations". *Journal of Vocational Behavior*, 4(2):223-235, 1974.

Rezek, J.R. "Dying and death". *Journal of Forensic Science*, 8:200-208, 1963.

Rhoads, Paul S. "Management of the patient with terminal illness". *Journal of the American Medical Association* 192:661-665, 1965.

Rhudick, P.H. and A.S. Dibner. "Age, personality and health correlates of death concerns in normal aged individuals". *Journal of Gerontology*, 16:44-49, 1961.

Rhudick, P.J. and A.S. Dibner. "Attitudes toward death in older persons: a symposium". *Journal of Gerontology*, 16:44-66, January, 1961.

Rich, T. et. al. "Attitudes of medical residents toward the dying patients in a general hospital". *Postgraduate Medicine*, 46:373-375, September, 1966.

Richmond, Julius B. and Harry A. Waisman. "Psychological aspects of management of children with malignant diseases". *American Journal of Diseases of Children*, 89(1):42-47, January, 1955.

Richter, Curt P. "On the phenomenon of sudden death in animals and man". *Psychosomatic Medicine*, 19(103):191-198, 1957.

Riegel, Klaus F., Ruth M. Riegel, and Gunther Meyer. "A study of the dropout rates in longitudinal research on aging and the prediction of death". *Journal of Personality and Social Psychology*, 5(3):343-348, 1967.

Ries, H. "An unwelcome child and her death instinct". *International Journal of Psychoanalysis*, 26:153-161, 1945.

Riga, Peter. "Euthanasia". *St. Anthony's Messenger*, 12-17, August, 1974.

"Right to live - or die. K. A. Quinlan case". *Time*,106:40+, October 27, 1975.

Rinear, Eileen R. "Helping the survivors of expected death". *Nursing*, 5:60-65, March, 1975.

Ristus, Ruth. "The loneliness of death". *The American Journal of Nursing*, 58:1283-1284, September, 1958.

Rizzo, R.F. and J.M. Yonder. "Eerie need to redefine death". *America*, 134:122-123, February 14, 1976.

Roberts, W.W. "The death instinct in morbid anxiety". *Journal of the Royal Army Medical Corps*, 81:61-73, 1943.

Robertson, J. "Some responses of young children to loss of maternal care". *Nursing Times*, 49:382, 1953.

Robertson, John A. and Norman Fost. "Passive euthanasia of defective newborn infants: legal considerations". *Journal of Pediatrics*, 88(5):883-889, May, 1976.

Rochlin, Gregory. "The loss complex: a contribution to the etiology of depression". *Journal of the American Psychoanalytical Association,* 7:299-316, 1959.

Rogers, William F. "Needs of the bereaved". *Pastoral Psychology,* 1:17-21, 1950.

Rogge, Louis. "The anointing of the sick in historical perspective". *Linacre Quarterly,* 42(3):205-213, 1975.

Rogo, D.S. "Parapsychology - its contribution to the study of death". *Omega: Journal of Death and Dying,* 5(2):99-114, 1974.

Roose, Lawrence. "The dying patient". *International Journal of Psychoanalysis,* 50:385-395, 1969.

Roose, Lawrence J. "To die alone". *Mental Hygiene,* 53:321-326, July, 1969.

Rose, M.S. "Who should choose". *Lancet,* 1:465-466, March, 1969.

Rosen, David H. "The serious suicide attempt". *Journal of the American Medical Association,* 235(19):2105-2109, May 10, 1976.

Rosenblatt, Paul C , Douglas A. Jackson, and Rose P. Walsh. "Coping with anger and aggression in mourning". *Omega: Journal of Death and Dying,* 3(4):271-284, 1972.

Rosenthal, Hattie. "The fear of death as an indispensable factor in psychotherapy". *American Journal of Psychotherapy,* 17:619-630, 1963.

Rosenthal. Hattie. "Psychotherapy for the dying". *American Journal of Psychotherapy,* 11:626-633, 1957.

Rosenthal Pauline. "The death of the leader in group psychotherapy". *American Journal of Orthopsychiatry,* 17:234-266, 1947.

Rosenwaile, Ira. "Seasonal variation of deaths in the United States, 1951-1960". *Journal of American Statistical Association,* 61(315):706-715, September, 1966.

Rosenzweig, Saul. "Sibling death as a psychological experience with reference to schizophrenia". *Psychoanalytic Review,* 30:177-186, 1943.

Rosenzweig, Saul and D. Bray. "Sibling deaths in anamnesis of schizophrenic parents". *Archives of Neurological Psychiatry,* 49:71-92, 1943.

Rosner, Albert. "Mourning before the fact". *Journal of the American Psychoanalytic Association*, 10:564-570, 1962.

Rosner, Aria C. "How we do it". *The Journal of School Health*, 44(8):455-457, 1974.

Rosoff, S. et. al. "The EEG in establishing brain death. A 10-year report with criteria and legal safeguards in the 50 states". *Electroencephalography and Clinical Neurophysiology*, 24:283-284, March, 1968.

Rothenberg, Albert. "Psychological problems in terminal cancer management". *Cancer*, 14:1063-1073, 1961.

Ruff, Frank. "Have we the right to prolong dying?". *Medical Economics*, 37:39-44, 1961.

Russell, Bertrand. "Your child and the fear of death". *The Forum*, 81:174-178, 1929.

Ryan, Patrick J. "Death on three continents". *America*, 133:348-350, November 22, 1975.

Rynearson, Edward H. "Symposium: what shall we tell the cancer patient? An internist's view". *Proceedings of the Staff Meetings of the Mayo Clinic*, 35:240-243, May 11, 1960.

Sabatini, Paul and Robert Kastenbaum. "The do-it-yourself death certificate as a research technique". *Life Threatening Behavior*, 3:20-32, 1973.

Sachs, Hans. "Beauty, life and death". *American Imago*, 1:81-133, 1940.

Sadler, A.M. et. al. "Transplantation and the law: progress toward uniformity". *New England Journal of Medicine*, 282:717-723, 1970.

Safran, Claire. "I don't intend to die this year". *Today's Health* 50(9):24-30, 1972.

St. John-Stevas, Norman. "Euthanasia". *America*, 132(21):421-422, May 31, 1975.

"Saints among us". *Time,* 106:47-49+, December 29, 1975.

Salter, Charles and Carlotta deLerma. "Attitudes towards aging and behavior toward the elderly among young people as a function of death anxiety". *The Gerontologist*, 16(3):232-236, June, 1976.

Sand, Patricia, Goodhue Livingston, and Robert G. Wright. "Psychological assessment of candidates for a hemodialysis program". *Annals of Internal Medicine*, 64:602-609, March, 1966.

Sandford, B. "Some notes on a dying patient". *International Journal of Psychoanalysis*, 38:158-165, 1957.

Sanua, Victor D. "A comparative study of schizophrenics of different socio-cultural backgrounds (Protestant, Irish, Catholic, and Jewish): parental loss and prognosis in terms of re-hospitalization". *Revista de Psicologia Normal e Patologica* 11:104-118, 1966.

Sarnoff, Irving and Seth M. Corwin. "Castration anxiety and the fear of death". *Journal of Personality*, 27:374-385, 1959.

Saul, Leon J. "Reactions of a man to natural death". *Psychoanalytic Quarterly*, 28:383-386, 1959.

Saul, Sidney and Shura Sidney. "Old people talk about death". *Omega: Journal of Death and Dying*, 4:27-35, 1973.

Saunders, Cicely. "Care of the dying: mental distress in the dying". *Nursing Times,* 55:1067-1068, October 30, 1959.

Saunders, Cicely. "Care of the dying: should a patient know . . .?". *Nursing Times,* 55:994-995, October 16, 1959.

Saunders, Cicely. "The care of the dying: the control of pain in terminal cancer". *Nursing Times,* 55:1031+, October 23, 1959.

Saunders, Cicely. "Care of the dying: the nursing of patients dying of cancer". *Nursing Times*, 55:1091-1092, November 6, 1959.

Saunders, Cicely. "Care of the dying: the problem of euthanasia". *Nursing Times*, 55:960-961, October, 1959.

Saunders, Cicely. "Care of the dying: when a patient is dying". *Nursing Times*, 55:1129-1130, November 13, 1959.

Saunders, C. "The management of fatal illness in childhood". *Proceedings of the Royal Society of Medicine*, 62:550-553, June, 1969.

Saunders, Cicely. "Death and responsibility: a medical director's view". *Psychiatric Opinion*, 3(4):28-34, August, 1966.

Saunders, Cicely. "The last stages of life". *American Journal of Nursing*, 65:70-75, March, 1965.

Saunders, Cicely. "The management of terminal illness". (Part 1.) *Hospital Medicine,* 225-228, December, 1966.

Saunders, Cicely. "The management of terminal illness". (Part 2.) *Hospital Medicine,* 317-320, January, 1967.

Saunders, Cicely. "The management of terminal illness". (Part 3.) *Hospital Medicine,* 433-436, February, 1967.

Saunders, Cicely. "The problem of euthanasia". *Nursing Times,* :960-961, October, 1959.

Saunders, Cicely. "The treatment of intractable pain in terminal cancer". *Proceedings of the Royal Society of Medicine,* 56(3):191-197, March, 1963.

Sautler, C. "The physician, the child and death. 3. The psychoanalytic approach". *Revue de Medecine Psychosomaticue et de Psychologie Medicale,* 10:425-429, October-December, 1968.

Sawa, M. "Standards for determining death. Cerebral death from the standpoint of the electroencephalogram". *Surgical Therapy,* 20:423-426, April, 1969.

Schaffer, H.R. and W.M. Callendar. "Psychological effects of hospitalization in infancy". *Pediatrics,* 24:528-539, 1959.

Scharfetter, F. "The signs of irrevocable death and the problem when resuscitation should be discontinued as hopeless". *Zeitschrift fur Allgemeinmedizin,* 45:830-834, 1969.

Scheils, Merrill and Susan Agrest. "Who was Karen Quinlan". *Newsweek,* 86(18):60, November 3, 1975.

Schein, Edgar. "Reaction patterns to severe, chronic stress in American Army prisoners of war of the Chinese". *Journal of Social Issues,* 13:21-30, 1957.

Schilder, Paul. "The attitude of murderers toward death". *Journal of Abnormal and Social Psychology,* 31:348-363, 1936.

Schilder, Paul and D. Wechsler. "The attitudes of children toward death". *Pedagogical Seminary and the Journal of Genetic Psychology,* 45:406-451, 1934.

Schillito, J., Jr. "The organ donor's doctor; a new role for the neurosurgeon". *New England Journal of Medicine,* 281:1070-1071, November 6, 1969.

Schleyer, F. "The value of the determination of time of death". *Beitraege zur Gerichtlichen Medizin,* 25:66-68, 1969.

Schmahl, Jane A. "Ritualism in nursing practice". *Nursing Forum,* 3:74-84, 1964.

Schmale, A.H. "Relationship of separation depression to disease". *Psychosomatic Medicine,* 20:259-277, 1958.

Schmale, A.H.J. and H.P. Iker. "The affect of hopelessness and the development of cancer. I. Identification of uterine cervical cancer in women with atypical cytology". *Psychosomatic Medicine,* 28:714, 1966.

Schmitt, R.C. "Death, disease and property taxes". *Hawaii Medical Journal*, 25:34-35, October, 1965.

Schnaper, N. "Care of the dying patient". *Medical Times*, 92:537-543, May, 1965.

Schneck, J.M. "Unconscious relationship between hypnosis and death". *Psychoanalytic Review*, 38:271-275, 1951.

Schneider, H. "Confirmation of brain death". *Deutsches Medizinishes Wochenschrift*, 94:2404-2405, November, 1969.

Schneider, H. "Criteria of the beginning of death". *Deffentliche Gesundheitwesen*, 31:536-541, November, 1969.

Scherlis, L. "Death: the diagnostic dilemma". *Maryland Medical Journal*, 17:77-78, December, 1968.

Schoenberg, B.B. et. al. "Physicians and the bereaved". *General Practitioner*, 40:105-108, October, 1969.

Schontz, Franklin C. and Stephen L. Fink. "A psychobiological analys s of discomfort, pain and death". *Journal of General Psychology*, 60 275-287, 1959.

Schrank, J. "Death: guide to books and audio-visual aids". *Media and Methods*, 7:32-54, 1971.

Schreiner, G.E. and J.F. Maher. "Hemodialysis for chronic renal failure. III. Medical, moral and ethical, and socio-economic problems". *Annals of Internal Medicine*, 62:551-557, 1965.

Schulz, Richard and Aderman, David. "Clinical research and the stages of dying". *Omega: Journal of Death and Dying*, 5(2):137-143, 1974.

Schupak, Eugene and John P. Merrill. "Experience with long-term interm ttent hemodialysis". *Annals of Internal Medicine*, 62:509-517, March, 1965.

Schur, Thomas J. "What man has told children about death". *Omega: Journal of Death and Dying*, 2:84-90, 1971.

Schurr, G.N. "Why bother about life beyond death?". *The Christian Century*, 83:424-426, April, 1966.

Schuyler, Dean. "Counseling suicide survivors: issues and answers". *Omega: Journal of Death and Dying*, 4(4):313-321, 1973.

Schuyler, Dean. "When was the last time you took a suicidal child to lunch?". *The Journal of School Health*, 43(8):504-506, 1973.

Scott, Bryon T. "Physicians' attitude survey". *Medical Opinion*, 3:32-34, 1974.

Scott, C.A. "Old age and death". *American Journal of Psychology*, 8:67-122, 1896.

Scott, W.C. "Mania and mourning". *International Journal of Psychoanalysis*, 45:373-379, April-July, 1964.

Scribner, B.H. "Presidential address: ethical problems of using artificial organs to maintain human life". *Transactions of the American Society of Artificial Internal Organs*, 10:209-212, 1964.

Searles, H. "Schizophrenia and the inevitability of death". *Psychiatric Quarterly*, 35:631-635, 1961.

Sebastian, Megan. "In time of sorrow you'll do the right thing". *Magazine of the Midlands* (Sunday, Omaha World Herald, Omaha, Nebraska), 4+, March 28, 1976.

"The second national congress on medical ethics". *Delaware Medical Journal*, 41:126-128, April, 1969.

Segal, Hanna. "Fear of death: notes on the analysis of an old man". *International Journal of Psychoanalysis*, 39:178-181, 1958.

Seiden, Richard H. "The problem of suicide on college campuses". *The Journal of School Health*, 41(5):243-248, 1971.

Seiden, Richard H. "Suicide capital? A study of the San Francisco suicide rate". *Bulletin of Suicidology*, 1-10, August, 1967.

Seiden, Richard H. "We're driving young blacks to suicide". *Psychology Today*, 4:24-28, August, 1970.

Seitz, Pauline M. and Louise H. Warrick. "Perinatal death: the grieving mother". *American Journal of Nursing*, 74(11):2028-2033, November, 1974.

Seldon, Elaine. ". . . Even the elderly". *R.N.*, 39(1):66-70, January, 1976.

Seliger, Susan. "Therapeutic funerals". *The National Observer*, 9, April 17, 1976.

Seligman, Martin E. "Submissive death: giving up on life". *Psychology Today*, 7:80-85, May, 1974.

Seligman, Roslyn et. al. "The effect of earlier parental loss in adolescence". *Archives of General Psychiatry*, 31:475-479, October, 1974.

Selvey, Carole. "Concerns about death in relation to sex, dependency, guilt about hostility and feelings of powerlessness". *Omega: Journal of Death and Dying*, 4:209-219, 1973.

Sepulveda, B. "Concept of death". *Gaceta Medica de Mexico*, 99:631-633, July, 1969.

Shands, Harley C. "Psychological mechanisms in cancer patients". *Cancer*, 4:1159-1170, 1951.

Shanks, Ann Zane. "I barely feel whole". *Today's Health*, 49(8):50-57, 1971.

Shapiro, H.A. "Brain death and organ transplantation". *Journal of Forensic Medicine*, 15:89-90, July-September, 1968.

Share, Lynda. "Family communication in the crisis of a child's fatal illness: a literature review and analysis". *Omega: Journal of Death and Dying*, 3(3):187-201, 1972.

Sharer, Lloyd. "Nothing sacred in Hollywood - not even funerals". *Parade*, 21+, December, 1964.

Sharp, D. "Lessons from a dying patient". *American Journal of Nursing*, 68:1517-1520, July, 1968.

Shaw, E.B. "Sudden unexpected death in infancy syndrome". *American Journal of Diseases of Children*, 116:115-119, August, 1968.

Shea, E.J. et. al. "Hemodialysis for chornic renal failure. IV. Psychological considerations". *Annals of Internal Medicine*, 62:558-563, 1965.

Sheatsley, Paul B. and Jacob J. Feldman "The assassination of President Kennedy: a preliminary report on public reactions and behavior". *Public Opinion Quarterly*, 28:189-215, 1964.

Sheperd, J. Barrie. "Ministering to the dying patient". *The Pulpit*, 9-12, July-August, 1966.

Sheps, J. "Management of fear of death in chronic disease". *Journal of the American Geriatric Society*, 5:793-797, 1957.

Sher, Byron D. "Funeral prearrangement: mitigating the undertaker's bargaining advantage". *Stanford Law Review*, 15:415-479, May, 1963.

Sherrill, Helen H. and Lewis J. Sherrill. "Interpreting death to children". *International Journal of Religious Education*, 28:4-6, October, 1951.

Sherwood, H.C. What every woman should know about her estate". *Harper's*, 108:105, November, 1974.

Shideler, M.M. "Coup de grace". *Christian Century*, 82:1499-1502, December, 1966.

Shneidman, E.S. "The Los Angeles suicide prevention center". *American Journal of Public Health*, 55(1):21-26, January, 1965.

Shneidman, E.S. "Orientation toward cessation: a reexamination of current modes of death". *Journal of Forensic Science*, 113:33-45, January, 1968.

Shneidman, E.S. et. al. "Comprehensive suicide prevention program". *California Mental Health Research Digest*, 37, 1965.

Shneidman, Edwin S. "Death questionnaire". *Psychology Today*, 4:67-72, August, 1970.

Shneidman, Edwin S. "The enemy". *Psychology Today*, 4:37-41, 62-66, August, 1970.

Shneidman, Edwin S. "On the deromanticization of death". *American Journal of Psychotherapy*, 25:4-17, 1971.

Shneidman, Edwin S. "Preventing suicide". *Bulletin of Suicidology*, 19-25, 1967.

Shneidman, Edwin S. "Suicide notes are dull". *Science Digest*, 76(5):77, November, 1974.

Shneidman, Edwin S. "Suicide, sleep and dearh". *Journal of Consulting Psychology*, 28:95-106, 1964.

Shneidman, Edwin S. "You and death". *Psychology Today*, 5:43-45, 74-80, June, 1971.

Shoor, Mervyn and Mary H. Speed. "Death, delinquency and the mourning process". *Psychiatric Quarterly*, 36:540-558, 1963.

Shoor, Mervyn and Mary H. Speed. "Delinquency as a manifestation of the mourning process". *Psychiatric Quarterly*, 37:540-558, 1963.

Shor, Ronald E. "A survey or representative literature on Freud's death-instinct hypothesis". *Journal of Humanistic Psychology*, 1:98-110, 1961.

Shrut, Samuel D. "Attitudes toward old age and death". *Mental Hygiene*, 42:259-266, 1958.

Siggins, L.C. "Mourning: a critical survey of the literature". *International Journal of Psychiatry*, 3:418-432, 1967.

Siggins, L.D. "Mourning: a critical survey of the literature". *International Journal of Psychoanalysis*, 47:14-25, 1966.

Silverman, D. "Cerebral death and the electroencephalogram. Report of the Ad Hoc Committee on the American Electroencephalographic Society on EEG Criteria for Determination of Cerebral Death". *Journal of the American Medical Association*, 209-1505-1510, September 8, 1969.

Silverman, P. and S. Englander. "The widow's view of her dependent children". *Omega: Journal of Death and Dying*, 6(1):3-21, 1975.

Silverman, Phyllis. "Factor involved in accepting an offer of help". *Archives of Thanatology*, 3:161ff, Fall, 1971.

Silverman, Phyllis R. "The widow as a caregiver in a program of preventive intervention with other widows". *Mental Hygiene*, 54(4):540-547, 1970.

Silverman, Phyllis R. "Widowhood and preventive intervention". *Family Coordinator*, 21:95, 1972.

Silverman, Phyllis R. and Cecile Strugnell. "The funeral director's wife as caregiver". *Omega: Journal of Death and Dying*, 2:174+, August, 1971.

Silverman, Phyllis Rolfe. "Services to the widowed: first steps in a program of preventive intervention". *Community Mental Health Journal*, 3(1):37-44, Spring, 1967.

Silverman, Phyllis Rolfe. "The widow-to-widow program: an experiment in preventive intervention". *Mental Hygiene*, 53:333-337, July, 1969.

Simmel, E. "Self-preservation and the death instinct". *Psychoanalytic Quarterly*, 13:160-185, 1944.

Simmons, Leo W. "Attitudes toward aging and the aged: primitive societies". *Journal of Gerontology*, 1(1):72-95, January, 1946.

Simpson, K. "The moment of death. A new medico-legal problem". *Acta Anesthesiological Scandinavica Supplement*, 29:361+, 1968.

Simpson, Michael A. "The do-it-yourself death certificate in evoking and estimating student attitudes toward death". *Journal of Medical Education*, 475-477, March, 1975.

Skelsie, Barbara M. "An exploratory study of grief in old age". *Smith College Studies in Social Work*, 45(2):159-182, February, 1975.

Slater, Jack. "Suicide: a growing menace to black women". *Ebony*, 28(11):152-160, September, 1973.

Smith, A.G. et. al. "The dying child. Helping the family cope with impending death". *Clinica Pediatrica*, 8:131-134, March, 1969.

Smith, Delos. "Winning against cancer: my own private war". *Reader's Digest*, 102(614):104-107, June, 1973.

Smith, Harmon. "Life be not proud". *Linacre Quarterly*, 42(3):168-175, 1975.

Smith, Walter. "Pastoral care of dying patients and their families". *Linacre Quarterly*, 42(3):199-205, August, 1975.

Snider, A.J. "Last rites, do they bring fear or reassurance?". *Science Digest*, 65:60-61, June, 1969.

Snider, Al. "Can death be postponed". *Science Digest*, 73(6):64, June, 1973.

Sobel, David E. "Death and dying". *American Journal of Nursing*, 74(1):98-99, January, 1974.

Solnit, A.J. and M. Green. "Psychological considerations in the management of deaths in pediatric hospital services: I, the doctor and the child's family". *Pediatrics*, 24:106-112, 1959.

Solnit, Albert J. "The dying child". *Developmental Medicine and Child Neurology*, 7:693-704, 1965.

Solnit, Albert J. and Morris Green. "Psychologic considerations in the management of deaths on pediatric hospital services". *Pediatrics*, 24(1):106-112, July, 1959.

Solow, Victor D. "I died at 10:52 A.M.". *Reader's Digest*, 105(630):170-182, October, 1974.

Somerville, R.M. "Death education as part of family life education: using imaginative literature for insights into family crisis". *Family Coordinator*, 20:223-224, 1971.

"Sometime soon - I will be dead of cancer". *Medical Insight*, 5(5):22-25, May, 1973.

Sommer, Carita. "Four distinctive views of the dying patient: managing the terminal care of herself". *RN*, 38(4):37-38, 1975.

Spann, W. "Definite concepts regarding legislation on the actual time of death". *Munchener Medizinische Wochenschrift*, 111:2253-2255, October 31, 1969.

Spilka, R., R.J. Pelligrini and K. Dailey. "Religion: American values and death perspective". *Sociological Symposium*, 1:57-66, 1968.

Spinetta, John J. "The dying child's awareness of death: a review". *Psychological Bulletin*, 81(4):256-260, 1974.

Spinetta, John J. and Lorrie J. Maloney. "Death anxiety in the outpatient leukemic child". *Pediatrics,* 56:103-107, December 1975.

Spinetta, John J., David Rigler, and Myron Karon. "Anxiety in the dying child". *Pediatrics*, 52(6):841-845, December, 1973.

Spinetta, John J., David Rigler, and Myron Karon. "Personal space as a measure of a dying child's sense of isolation". *Journal of Consulting and Clinical Psychology* 42(6):751-756, December, 1974.

Spitzer, Stephan P. and Jeannette R. Folta. "Death in the hospital: a problem for study". *Nursing Forum,* 3:85-92, 1964.

Srivastava, M.L. "Relationship between the birth rate and the death rate in stable populations with the same fertility but different mortality schedules". *Eugenics Quarterly,* 13:231-239, September, 1966.

Stacey, C.L. and K. Marken. "The attitudes of college students and penitentiary inmates toward death and a future life". *Psychiatric Quarterly* (Supplement), 26:27-32, 1952.

Stacey, C.L. and Marie L. Richen. "Attitudes toward death and future life among normal and subnormal adolescent girls". *Exceptional Children,* 20:259-262, 1954.

Staff, Clement. "Death is no outsider". *Psychoanalysis,* 2:56-70, 1953.

Star, Cima and Sheri Steiner. "Why more women are committing suicide". *McCalls,* 103(4):47, January, 1976.

"Staring death in the face". *Science Digest,* 79:10, May, 1976.

Steinbereithner, K. "Border areas between life and death. Anesthesiological problems". *Wiener Klinische Wochenschrift,* 81:530-533, July 18, 1969.

Stekhoven, W. "Professor Van den Berg's plea for active euthanasia". *Nederlands Tijdschrift voor Genecskunde,* 113:1358-1360, August 2, 1969.

"Steps to suicide". *Science Digest,* 78:24, September, 1975.

Sterba, Richard. "On Halloween". *American Imago,* 5:213-224, 1948.

Stern, Karl, Gwendolyn M. Williams and Miguel Prados. "Grief reactions in later life". *American Journal of Psychiatry,* 108:289-293, 1951.

Stern, M.M. "Fear of death and neurosis". *Journal of the American Psychoanalytic Association,* 16:3-31, January, 1968.

Stern, Winokur et. al. "Alterations in physiological measures during experimentally induced attitudes". *Journal of Psychosomatic Research,* 5:73-82, 1961.

Sternglass, E.J. "Infant mortality and nuclear tests". *Bulletin of the Atomic Scientists*, 25:18-20, April, 1969.
Stevens, A.C. "Facing death". *Nursing Times*, 58:777-779, 1962.
Stevens, L.A. "When is death". *Reader's Digest*, 94:225+, May, 1969.
Stewart, D.R. "Message of the kite". *Reader's Digest*, 95:122, July, 1969.
Still, J.W. "To be or not to be--alive or dead?". *Journal of the American Geriatrical Society*, 17:522-524, May, 1969.
Stitt, Abby. "Emergency after death". *Emergency Medicine*, March, 1971.
Stojic, B. "Is a man who is pulseless and has stopped breathing dead?". *Medical Journal of Australia*, 2:571, September 13, 1969.
Stokes, A. "On resignation". *International Journal of Psychosomatics*, 43:175-181, 1962.
Stolnitz, G.J. "Recent mortality trends in Latin America, Asia and Africa". *Population Studies*, 19(2):117-138, November, 1965.
Storlie, Frances. "Gloria". *American Journal of Nursing*, 75(7):1188-1190, July, 1975.
Strauss, A. and B. Glaser. "The social loss dying patients". *American Journal of Nursing*, 64(6):119-121, January, 1964.
Strauss, Anselm L., Barney Glaser, and Jeanne C. Quint. "The non-accountability of terminal care". *Hospitals*, 38:73-87, 1964.
Strauss, Richard H. "I think, therefore". *Perspectives in Biology and Medicine*, 8(4):516-517, Summer, 1965.
Stringfellow, Marvin E. "Talking about suicide". *School Health Review*, 5(5):40, 1974.
Stumpf, Samuel Enoch. "Some moral dimensions of medicine". *Annals of Internal Medicine*, 64:460-470, February, 1966.
Suarez, R.M. et. al. "Morbidity and mortality in aged Puerto Ricans". *Journal of American Geriatric Society*, 13:805-814, 1965.
"Sudden death in young adults". *Journal of the American Medical Association*, 203:138, January 8, 1968.
"Sudden unexpected death". *Journal of the American Medical Association*, 209:1358, September 1, 1969.

Sugar, Max. "Adolescent depression related to mourning processes". *Roche Report. Frontiers of Clinical Psychiatry*, 4:3, February 15, 1967.
"Suicide in children". *British Medical Journal*, 1(5958):592, March 15, 1975.
"Suicide wish among divorcees". *Intellect*, 104(2373):418-419, March, 1976.
Sumner, Francis B. "A biologist reflects upon old age and death". *Scientific Monthly*, 61:143, 1945.
Sutter, J. et. al. "Lethal equivalents and demographic measures of mortality". *Symposia on Quantitative Biology*, 29:41-50, 1964.
Sutton, G.F. "Hospitalization in the last year of life. United States, 1961". *Vital Health Statistics, National Center Statistics*, 22:1-46, September, 1965.
Swenson, Wendell M. "Attitudes toward death among the aged". *Minnesota Medicine*, 42:399-402, 1959.
Swenson, Wendell M. "Attitudes toward death in an aged population". *Journal of Gerontology*, 16:49-52, 1961.
Swenson, Wendell M. "The psychology of aging: its significance in the practice of geriatric medicine". *Postgraduate Medicine*, 34:89-93, July, 1963.
Tachibana, N. "Life, death and the anesthesiologist". *Naika*, 23:845-849, May, 1969.
Takeshita, H. et al. "Problems of 'brain death' ". *Japenese Journal of Anesthesiology*, 18:277-284, April, 1969.
Takeuchi, K. "Standards for determining death. Cerebral death from the standpoint of the neurosurgeon". *Surgical Therapy*, 20:433-444, April, 1969.
"A tale of two hospitals - cause of death: bureaucracy". *Prism*, 3(6):22-26, June, 1975.
Tarnower, W. "The dying patient: psychological needs of the patient, his family and the physician". *Nebraska Medical Journal*, 54:6-10, January, 1969.
Teicher, J.D. " 'Combat fatigue' or death anxiety neurosis". *Journal of Nervous and Mental Disease*, 117:234-243, 1953.
Templer, D.I. "Construction and validation of death anxiety scale". *Journal of General Psychology*, 82:176-177, 1970.
Templer, Donald. "Death anxiety in religiously very involved persons". *Psychological Reports*, 31:361-362, 1972.

"Test of friendship". *RN*, 34(10):42+, October, 1971.

Thaler, Otto F. "Grief and depression". *Nursing Forum*, 5:8-22, 1966.

"Thanatology: death and modern man". *Time*, 84:92, November 20, 1964.

"The Need for Education on Death and Suicide". *Journal of School Health*, 39(4):270-274, April, 1969.

"The Sociology of Death," *Sociological Symposium,* 1:1-98, Fall, 1968.

"This may be mother's last Christmas". *Today's Health*, 52(7):38-42, July, 1974.

Thomas, Hwu. "The psychological approach to cremation". *The Funeral Director*, 697-703, December, 1966.

Thomas, John R. "Marguerite and me". *Pilgrimage*, 1:35ff, Fall-Winter, 1972.

Throckmorton, B.J. "Do Christians believe in death?". *The Christian Century*, 96:998, July 23, 1969.

Tichauer, Ruth W. "Aspects of death and dying. Anthropology: Attitudes towards death and dying among the Aymara Indians of Bolivia". *Journal of the American Medical Women's Association*, 19(6):463-466, June, 1964.

"Time perspective and bereavement". *Omega*, 1(2): _____ , June, 1966.

Timmons, May. "Is it so awful?". *American Journal of Nursing*, 75(6):988, June, 1975.

"To secure methods for diagnosis of brain death". *Lakartidningen*, 66:2754, July 2, 1969.

Toole, J.F. "The neurologist and the concept of brain death". *Perspectives of Biological Medicine*, 14:599-607, 1971.

Tooley, Kay, "The choice of a surviving sibling as 'scapegoat' in some cases of maternal bereavement". *Journal of Child Psychology and Psychiatry*, 16:331-339, 1975.

Torre, Marie. "Edie Adams: how I survived". *Redbook*, 119:46-47, September, 1962.

Townes, Brenda, David A. Wold and Thomas H. Holmes. "Parental adjustment to childhood leukemia". *Journal of Psychosomatic Research*, 18(1):9-14, 1974.

Townsend, J.D. "Review of P.E. Irion's 'Funeral: vestige or value' ". *The Christian Century*, 83:369, March, 1966.

Treaton, Jean-Rene. "Discussion of a symposium on attitudes toward death in older persons". *Journal of Gerontology*, 16:44, 1961.

Treloar, Alan E. "The enigma of cause of death". *Journal of the American Medical Association*, 162(15):1376-1379, December 8, 1956.

Treuhaft, Decca. "St. Peter, don't you call me: American burial standards: classy expensive". *Frontier*, 3-10, November, 1958.

Trevor, Beeson. "Sacrificial suicides". *Christian Century*, 91:836-837, September 18, 1974.

Turczynowski, R. et. al. "Birth and death certificates as a source of information on the causes of death in past centuries". *Archives of Historical Medicine*, 31:213-219, 1968.

"Two views of the issue. The right to die - should a doctor decide?". *U.S. News and World Report*, 79(18):53-54, November 3, 1975.

Ueda, J. et. al. "Round table discussion: determination of death, information for clinicians". *Naika*, 23:870-887, May, 1969.

Ufema, Joy K. "Dare to care for the dying". *American Journal of Nursing*, 76(1):88-90, 1976.

Ujhely, Gertrud B. "Grief and depression: implications for preventive and therapeutic nursing care". *Nursing Forum*, 5:23-35, 1966.

Upsurge in suicides and ways to prevent them". *U.S. News and World Report*, 77(1):47-48, July 1, 1974.

Vaisrub, Samuel. "Dying is worked to death". *Journal of the American Medical Association*, 229(14):1909-1910, September 30, 1974.

Valdes-Dapena, Marie A. "Infant death syndrome". *Florida's Health*, 68(4): _____ , April, 1976.

Van Eys, J. "Suportive care for the child with cancer". *Pediatric Clinic of North America*, 215-224, February, 1976.

Vanden Bergh, R.L. "Let's talk about death to overcome inhibiting emotions". *American Journal of Nursing*, 66:71-73, January, 1966.

Veatch, R. and E. Wakin. "Death and dying". *U.S. Catholic*, 37:6-13, April, 1972.

Vernick, Joel and K. Myron. "Who's afraid of death on a leukemia ward?". *American Journal of Diseases of Children*, 109:393-397, 1965.

Vernon, Glenn. "Death control". *Omega: Journal of Death and Dying*, 3:131-138, 1972.

Verwoerdt, Adriaan. "Chronic ailments: communication with the fatally ill". *Chronic Ailments*, 15:105-111, May-June, 1965.

Verwoerdt, Adriaan. "Comments on: 'communication with the fatally ill' ". *Omega: Journal of Death and Dying*, 2(1):10-11, 1967.

Verwoerdt, Adriaan. "Communication with the fatally ill". *CA, A Cancer Journal for Clinicians*, 103-111, May-June, 1962.

Verwoedt, Adriaan. "Death and the family". *Medical Opinion and Review*, 1(12):38-43, 1966.

Verwoedt, Adriaan and Ruby Wilson. "Communication with fatally ill patients". *American Journal of Nursing*, 67(11):2307-2309, November, 1967.

Viorst, Judith. "Let us talk about death". *Redbook*, 141:33-4, June, 1973.

"Vital bouyancy of optimism: study by D. Phillips". *Time*, 94:55+, September 5, 1969.

Vitanza, Angelo A. "Toward a theory of crying". *Psychoanalysis and the Psychoanalytic Review*, 47:2-16, 1960-61.

"The voices of silence". *Time*, 97(1):68, July 6, 1970.

Vollen, Karen Helm and Charles G. Watson. "Suicide in relation to time of day and day of week". *American Journal of Nursing*, 75(2):263, February, 1975.

Vollman, Rita et. al. "The reaction of family systems to sudden and unexpected death". *Omega: Journal of Death and Dying*, 2:101-106, 1971.

Von Hug-hellmuth, Hermine. "The child's concept of death". *Psychoanalytic Quarterly*, 34:499-516, 1965.

Von Lerchenthal, Erich. "Death from psychic causes". *Bulletin of the Menninger Clinic*, 12:31-36, 1948. .

Vorreith, M. et. al. "Causes of death in the Army". *Vojenske Zdravotnicke Listy*, 34:240-243, December, 1965.

Wagner, Bernice M. "Teaching students to work with the dying". *American Journal of Nursing*, 64:128-131, November, 1964.

Wahl, Charles. "Bolstering the defenses of dying patients". *Hospital Physician*, 5:160+, March, 1969.

Wahl, Charles. "Helping the dying patient and his family". *Journal of Pastoral Care*, 26:93-98, 1972.

Wahl, Charles W. "The fear of death". *Bulletin of the Menninger Clinic*, 22:214-223, 1958.

Wahl, Charles W. "The physician's management of the dying patient". *Current Psychiatric Therapy*, 2:127-136, 1962.
Wahl, Charles W. "Suicide as a magical act". *Bulletin of the Menninger Clinic*, 21:91-98, May, 1957.
Wainwright, L. "Profound lesson for the living: seminar at University of Chicago's Billings Hospital". *Life*, 67:36-43, November 21, 1969.
Walkenstein, Eileen. "The death experience in insulin coma treatment". *American Journal of Psychiatry*, 112:985-990, 1956.
Walker, A.E. "The death of a brain". *Johns Hopkins Medical Journal*, 124:190-201, April, 1969.
Walker, J.V. "Attitudes to death". *Gerontologia Clinica*, 10:304-308, 1968.
Wallace, E. and B.D. Townes. "Dual role of comforter and bereaved: reactions of medical personnel to the dying child and his parents". *Mental Hygiene*, 53:372-332, July, 1969.
Wallace, L. "Death and the nurse". *Nursing Monthly*, 128:22, February 28, 1969.
Wallace, L. "The needs of the dying". *Nursing Times*, 65:1450-1451, November 13, 1969.
Wallace, M.A. "Nurse in suicide prevention". *Nursing Outlook*, 15:55-57, March, 1967.
Wallden, L. "Human dignity, healing art and care of the dying". *Lakartidningen* 62:3113-3117, September, 1965.
Walters, M. "Psychic death: report of a possible case". *Archives of Neurology and Psychiatry*, 52(1):84, 1944.
Walters, Orville S. "A Christian approach to death". *Light and Life*, March 18, 1975.
Waltzer, Herbert and Leon D. Hankoff. "One year's experience with a suicide prevention telephone service". *Community Mental Health Journal*, 1(4):309-315, Winter, 1965.
Wamsley, Frank X. "How to cope with the high cost of dying". *RN Magazine*, 37(8):57, August, 1974.
Warbasse, James Peter. "On life and death and immortality". *Zygon - Journal of Religion and Science*, 1(4):366-372, December, 1966.
Waugh, Evelyn. "Death in Hollywood". *Life Magazine*, 23:73-85, 1947.

Waxenberg, Sheldon E. "The importance of the communication of feeling about cancer". *New York Academy of Science Annals*, 125:1000-1005, 1966.

Weber, Leonard J. "Ethics and euthanasia; another view". *American Journal of Nursing*, 73:1228-1231, July, 1973.

Wecht, C. "Four views of organ transplants. Attorney describes current efforts to establish uniform guidelines". *Hospitals*, 43:54-57, November, 1969.

Weikel, Charles P. "The life you can save". *Harvest Years*, 10(1):6-11, January, 1970.

Weiner, H.B. "Living experiences with death - a journeyman's view through psychodrama". *Omega: Journal of Death and Dying*, 6(3):251-274, 1975.

Weisman, A.D. "Apropriate death". *International Journal of Psychiatry*, 2:190, 1966.

Weisman, A.D. "How shall a physician learn about death?". *Archives of Foundation of Thanatology*, 1:1-7, 1969.

Weisman, A.D. "Misgivings and misconceptions in the psychiatric care of terminal patients". *Psychiatry*, 33(1):67-84, 1970.

Weisman, A.D. "On the value of denying death". *Pastoral Psychology*, 23:24-32, June, 1972.

Weisman, A.D. "Partial grief and total bereavement". *Journal of Geriatric Psychiatry*, 4:23-25, 1970.

Weisman, A.D. "The right way to die". *Psychiatry and Social Science Review*, 2(12):2-7, 1968.

Weisman, Avery and Arthur H. Becker. "The patient with a fatal illness - to tell or not to tell". *Journal of the American Medical Association*, 201(8):646-648, August, 1967.

Weisman, Avery D. "Birth of a death-people". *Omega: Journal of Death and Dying*, 1(1):3-4, March, 1966.

Weisman, Avery D. "Coping with untimely death". *Psychiatry* 36(4):366-378, 1973.

Weisman, Avery D. "Death and responsibility: a psychiatrist's view". *Psychiatric Opinion*, 3(4):22-26, 1966.

Weisman, Avery D. and Thomas P. Hackett. "The dying patient". *Forest Hospital Publications* (Des Plaines, Ill.), 1:16-21, 1962.

Weisman, Avery D. and Thomas P. Hackett. "Predilection to death". *Psychosomatic Medicine*, 23:232-256, 1961.

Weiss, Soma. "Instantaneous 'physiologic' death". *New England Journal of Medicine*, 223(20):793-797, November 4, 1940.

Wenkart, A. "Death in life". *Journal of Existence*, 7:75-90, 1968.

Wentzel, Kenneth B. "The dying are the living". *American Journal of Nursing*, 76(6):956-957, June, 1976.

Wessel, Morris. "A death in the family. The impact on children". *Journal of the American Medical Association*, 234(8):865-866, November 24, 1975.

West, Norman D. "The psychology of death in geriatrics". *Journal of the American Geriatrics Society*, 20(7):340-342, 1972.

West, Norman D. and Margaret A. Walsh. "Child's response to death loss". *Nebraska Medical Journal* 60:228-233, 1975.

Westercamp, Twilla. "Suicide". *American Journal of Nursing*, 75(2):260-262, February, 1975.

"When do we let the patient die?". *Annals of Internal Medicine*, 68:695-700, March, 1968.

"When should life be prolonged? K.A. Quinlan case". *Science News*, 108:213-214, October 4, 1975.

"When your wife is a widow what then". *Changing Times*, 25:6-9, June, 1971.

Whetmore, Robert. "The role of grief in psychoanalysis". *International Journal of Psychoanalysis*, 44:97-103, 1963.

Whisman, Sandra. "Four distinctive views of the dying patient: 'turn off the respirator and let Danny die' ". *RN*, 38(4):34-35, 1975.

White, Douglas. "An undergraduate course in death". *Omega: Journal of Death and Dying*, 1:167-174, 1970.

White, R.B. and L.T. Gatham. "The syndrome of ordinary grief". *AFP*, 8(2):96-104, August, 1973.

Whitman, Helen H. and Lukes, J. Shelby. "Behavior modification for terminally ill patients". *American Journal of Nursing*, 75(1):98-101, 1975.

Wiener, Jerry. "What should the child know of death". *Medical Insight*, 5(4):25-28, April, 1973.

Wilders, James G. "Should the cancer patient be told?". *Journal of the American Medical Association*, 200(8):733, May, 1967.

Wilkiemeyer, Diana S. "Affection: key to care for the elderly". *American Journal of Nursing*, 72(12):2166-2168, 1972.

William, J.S., Jr. "Infant and child mortality in Burma by Ethnic Group". *Eugenics Quarterly* 13:128-132, June, 1966.

Williams, H. "On teaching hospital's responsibility to counsel parents concerning their child's death". *Medical Journal of Australia,* 2:643-645, 1963.

Williams, Jane C. "Understanding the feelings of the dying". *Nursing,* 6(3):52-56, 1976.

Williams, M. "Changing attitudes to death, a survey of contributions in *Psychological Abstracts* over a thirty-year period". *Human Relations,* 19:405-423, 1966.

Williams, Mary. "The fear of death, part II. The fear of death in consciousness". *Journal of Analysis Psychology,* 7:29, 1962.

Williams, R.H. "Our role in the generation, modificiation and termination of life". *Archives of Internal Medicine,* 132:215, 1969.

Wilson, George R. "The sense of danger and the fear of death". *The Monist,* 13:352, 1902-1903.

Wilson, Robert N. "The social structure of a general hospital". *The Annals of the American Academy of Political and Social Science,* 346:67-76, March, 1963.

Winick, Charles. "Personality characteristics of embalmers". *Personnel and Guidance Journal,* 43(3):262-266, November, 1964.

Wise, Doreen. "Learning about dying". *Nursing Outlook,* 22:42-44, 1974.

Wiseman, Mark Harrington. "Death with thanks". *Harper's,* 249(1495):45-46, December, 1974.

Wittgenstein, G. "Fear of dying and of death as a requirement of the maturation process in man". *Hippocrates,* 31:765-769, 1960.

Wittner, Dale. "Life or death". *Today's Health,* 52(3):48-53, 1974.

Wodnisky, Abraham. "Psychiatric consultation with nurses on a leukemia service". *Mental Hygiene,* 48:282-287, 1964.

Wohlford, Paul. Extension of personal time, affective states, and expectation of personal death". *Journal of Personality and Social Psychology,* 3:559-566, 1966.

Wolf, Zane R. "What patients awaiting kidney transplants want to know". *American Journal of Nursing,* 76(1):92-94, 1976.

Wolff, Sula. "How children respond to death". *New Society,* 13:479-482, March, 1969.

Wolff, K. "Personality type and reaction toward aging and death". *Geriatrics,* 21:189-192, August, 1966.

Wolff, Kurt H. "A partial analysis of student reaction to President Roosevelt's death". *Journal of Social Psychology*, 26:35-53, 1947.

"Women top men in survival after midlife". *Geriatrics*, 24(7):52, 1969.

Woodruff, M.F.A. "Ethical problems in organ transplantation". *British Medical Journal*, 1:1457-1460, 1964.

Woodward, Kenneth L. "Life after death". *Newsweek*, 88:41, July 12, 1976.

World Medical Association. "Declaration of Helsinki: recommendations guiding doctors in clinical research". *World Medical Journal*, 11:281, 1964.

Wren-Lewis, John. "Breaking the final taboo". *Psychology Today*, 8(12):14-15, May, 1975.

Wretmark, G. "A study of grief reactions". *Acta Psychiatrica Neurologica Scandinavica Supplement*, 136:292, 1959.

Wrigley, J.R. "Critical questions in medical transplants". *America*, 120:334-337, March 22, 1969.

Wright, Robert G., Patricia Sand and Goodhue Livingston. "Psychological stress during hemodialysis for chronic renal failure". *Annals of Internal Medicine*, 64:611-620, March, 1966

Wylie, Max. "Living with grief". *Family Health*, 2:38-41, March, 1970.

Yalon, I. "Observations on mourning". *New Physician*, 13:80-81, March, 1964.

Yamamoto, Joe et. al. "Mourning in Japan". *American Journal of Psychiatry*, 125:1660-1665, 1969.

Yamazaki, S. "The physical attitudes of youths toward death". *Japanese Journal of Psychology*, 15:469-475, 1940.

Young, Michael et. al. "The mortality of widowers". *The Lancet* 2:254-256, 1963.

Young, William H. "Death of a patient during psychotherapy". *Psychiatry*, 23:103-108, 1960.

Yudkin, S. "Children and death". *Lancet*, 1:37-41, January, 1967.

Zazzaro, Joanne. "Death be not distorted". *Nation's Schools*, 91:1973:39-43, 102, 1973.

Zeligs, Rose. "Death casts its shadow on a child". *Mental Hygiene*, 51:9-20, January, 1907.

Zeligs, Rose, "Death is a part of life". *California Parent-Teacher*, 36:7, 1959.

Zeligs, Rose. "Judy learns about death". *California Parent-Teacher*, 41:6-7, 1964.

Zilboorg, Gregory. "Differential diagnostic types of suicide". *Archives of Neurology and Psychiatry*, 35(2):270-291, February, 1936.

Zilboorg, Gregory, "Fear of death". *Psychoanalytic Quarterly*, 12:465-475, 1943.

Zinker, Joseph C. and Stephen L. Fink. "The possibility for psychological growth in a dying person". *The Journal of General Psychology*, 74:185-199, April, 1966.

Ziskind, Eugene. "Isolation stress in medical and mental illness". *The Journal of the American Medical Association*, 168:1427-1430, November, 1958.

Zopf, Delores. "The dying patient, meeting his needs could be easier than you think". *Nursing*, 5:16, March, 1975.

BOOKS

Agee, James. *A death in the family*. New York: McDowell, Obolensky, 1957.

Ainsworth, Mary D. et. al. *Deprivation of maternal care*. New York: Schocken, 1966.

Alcott, Louisa M. *Little men*. New York: The MacMillan Co., 1963. Children's book.

Alcott, Louisa M. *Little women*. New York: World, 1969. Children's book.

Alden, Henry Mills. *A study of death*. New York: Harper & Brothers, 1895.

Allen, Charles L. *When you lose a loved one*. Westwood, New Jersey: F.H. Revell Co., 1959.

Allen, R. Earl. *Memorial messages*. Nashville, Tennessee: Broadman Press, 1964.

Allport, Gordon. *The individual and his religion*. New York: The MacMillan Company, 1950.

Alsop, Stewart. *Stay of execution: a sort of memoir*. Philadelphia: J.B. Lippincott Co., 1973.

Alvarez, A. *The savage God*. New York: Random House, 1972.

American blue book of funeral directors. New York: Kates-Boylston Publications, 1970-71.

American Medical Association. *Standard nomenclature of diseases and operations*. 4th ed. Philadelphia: Blakiston, 1952.

Anderson, Colena M. *Joy beyond grief*. Grand Rapids, Michigan: Zondervan Publishing House, 1971.

Anderson, Dorothy B. and L.J. McClean. *Identifying suicide potential*. New York: Human Sciences Pr., 1971.

Anthony, Sylvia. *The child's discovery of death*. New York: Harcourt, Brace & Co., 1940.

Aries, Philippe. *Western attitudes toward death: from the middle ages to the present*. Baltimore, Maryland: The John Hopkins University Press, 1974.

Armstrong, William H. *Sour land*. New York: Harper and Row Publishers, 1971.

Arnstein, Helene S. *What to tell your child about birth, illness, death, divorce and other family crises*. Indianapolis: The Bobbs-Merrill Co., Inc., 1960.

Autton, N. *The pastoral care of the dying*. London: S.P.C.K., 1966.

Bachmann, C. Charles. *Ministering to the grief sufferer*. Engelwood Cliffs, New Jersey: Prentice-Hall, Inc., 1964.

Baerwald, Reuben C. comp. *Hope in grief*. St. Louis, Missouri: Concordia Publishing House, 1966.

Bakan, David. *Disease, pain and sacrifice*. Chicago: University of Chicago Pr., 1968.

Bakan, David. *The duality of human existence*. Chicago: Rand, McNally & Co., 1966.

Baker, G.W. and D.W. Chapman ed. *Man and society in disaster*. New York: Basic Books, 1962.

Baker, Laura Nelson. *Cousin Tyrg*. Philadelphia: Lippincott, 1966.

Ball, Zachary. *Bristle face*. New York: Holiday House, 1962. Children's book.

Bane, J.Donald et. a . ed. *Death and the ministry*. New York: Schocken Books, 1975.

Barish, Louis and Rebecca Barish. *Basic Jewish beliefs*. New York: Jonathan David, Publishers, Inc., 1961.

Bartoli, Jennifer. *Nonna*. New York: Harvey House, 1975. Children's book.

Bataille, Georges. *Death and sensuality*. New York: Ballantine Books, 1969.

Bayless, Raymond. *The other side of death*. New Hyde Park, New York: University Books, Inc., 1971.

Bayley, Joseph. *How silently, how silently*. Elgin, Illinois: David C. Cook Publishing Co., 1968.

Bayley, Joseph. *The view from the hearse*. New York: Pyramid Publications, 1972.

Beable, William H. *Epitaphs: graveyard humor and eulogy*. New York: Thomas Y. Crowell, 1925.

Beauvoir, Simone de. *A very easy death*. New York: Warner Communications Co., 1972.

Beck, Frances. *Diary of a widow*. Boston: Beacon Pr., 1965.

Becker, Ernest. *The denial of death*. New York: The Free Press, 1973.

Becker, H. et. al. *Boys in white*. Chicago: University of Chicago Pr., 1961.

Becque, Maurice and Louis Becque. *Life after death*. New York: Hawthorn Books, Inc., 1960.

Bedau, Hugo Adam ed. *The death penalty in America*. Garden City, New York: Doubleday & Co., Inc., 1964.

Behnke, John A. and Sissela Bok ed. *The dilemmas of euthanasia*. Garden City, New York: Doubleday, 1975.

Beim, Jerrold. *With Dad alone*. New York: Harcourt, Brace and Co., 1954. Children's book.

Bell, Thomas. *In the midst of life*. New York: Atheneum Publishers, 1961.

Bellack, L. ed. *Handbook of community psychiatry and community mental health*. New York: Grune and Stratton, 1964.

Belleau, Wilfred E. *Funeral-service as a career*. Rev. ed. Angwin, California: Park Publishing House, 1968.

Benchley, Nathaniel. *Only earth and sky last forever*. New York: Harper and Row Publishers, 1975.

Bendann, Effie. *Death customs; an analytical study of burial rites*. 1st ed. Reprint. London: Dawsons, 1969.

Bender, David L. ed. *Problem of death: opposing viewpoints series*. Anoka, Minnesota: Greenhaven Press, 1974.

Bendit, Laurence J. *The mirror of life and death*. Wheaton, Illinois: Theosophical Pub. House, c1965.

Bergman, Abraham and Judith Choate. *Why did my baby die: the phenomenon of sudden infant death syndrome and how to cope with it*. New York: Joseph Okpaku Publishing Co., Inc., 1975.

Bermann, Eric. *Scapegoat; the impact of death-fear on an American family*. Ann Arbor: University of Michigan Pr., 1973.
Bernard, Hugh Y. *Law of death and disposal of the dead*. Dobbs Ferry, New York: Oceana Publications, 1966.
Bernardo, Felix. *Death, Bereavement and Widowhood: A Selected Bibliography*. Department of Sociology, University of Florida, Gainesville, Florida.
Bernstein, A. *Intern's manual (Cook County Hospital)*. Chicago: Year Book Medical Publishers, Inc., 1959.
Bettelheim, Bruno. *The empty fortress*. New York: Free Pr., 1967.
Blackwood, Andrew. *The funeral: sourcebook for ministers*. Grand Rapids, Michigan: Baker Book House, 1972.
Blaine, Graham B., Jr. *Youth and the hazards of affluence*. New York: Harper & Row, 1966.
Bliss, Harry A. *Modern tablets and sarcophogi*. Buffalo: H.A. Bliss, 1923.
Blocker, Henri. *Suicide*. Downers Grove, Illinois: Inter-varsity Press, 1973.
Blue, Rose. *Grandma didn't wave back*. New York: Franklin Watts, Inc., 1972.
Blum, R.H. et. al. *The management of the doctor-patient relationship*. New York: McGraw-Hill Book Co., 1960.
Book of the dead. 2d ed. New York: Barnes and Noble, 1949.
Bookstaber, David. *The idea of the development of the soul in medieval Jewish philosophy*. Philadelphia: Maurice Jacobs, 1950.
Boros, Ladislaus. *The mystery of death*. New York: Herder and Herder, 1965.
Bowers, Margaretta K. *Counseling the dying*. New York: Thomas Nelson & Sons, 1964.
Bowlby, J. *Attachment and loss*. V. 1, *Attachment*. New York: Basic Books, 1969.
Bowlby, J. *Attachment and loss*. V. 2, *Separation*. New York: Basic Books, 1973.
Bowlby, J. *Grief and mourning in infancy*. New York: Universities Pr., 1960.
Bowlby, John. *Childhood mourning and its implications for psychiatry*. New York: International University Pr., 1972.

Bowlby, John. *Maternal care and mental health*. New York: Schocken, 1966.

Bowman, LeRoy. *The American funeral*. Westport, Connecticut: Greenwood Press, 1959, 1973.

Bowman, Leroy. *The American Funeral: A Way of Death*. New York: Paperback Library, 1964.

Brandon, S.G.F. *The judgement of the dead: the idea of life after death in the major religions*. New York: Charles Scribner's Sons, 1969.

Brim, Orville G., Jr. et al. *Death and medical conduct*. New York: Russell Sage Foundation, 1969.

Brim, Orville G., Jr. *The dying patient*. New York: Russell Sage Foundation, 1970.

Brindly, William and Samuel Weatherly. *Ancient sepulchral monuments*. London: Brooks, Day and Son, 1937.

Bro, Marguerite H. *When children ask*. New York: Harper and Brothers, 1956.

The Brothers of St. Joseph. *To bury the dead*. Bethany, Oklahoma: The Brothers of St. Joseph, 1963.

Brothwell, Don R. *Digging up bones: the excavation, treatment and study of human skeletal remains*. London: The British Museum, 1963.

Brown, John M. *Morning faces*. New York: McGraw-Hill Book Co., 1949.

Brown, Margaret W. *The dead bird*. New York: Young Scott Books, 1958. Children's book.

Brown, Norman. *Life against death*. Middletown, Connecticut: Wesleyan University Press, 1959.

Browne, Sir Thomas. *Urne Buriall and the garden of Cyrus*. Cambridge, England: University Press, 1958.

Buck, Pearl. *The beech tree*. New York: John Day, 1955. Children's book.

Buck, Pearl S. *The big wave*. New York: The John Day Co., 1947.

Buck, Pearl S. *The good earth*. New York: The John Day Co., 1931.

Budge, Ernest A. *The mummy: chapters on Egyptian funeral archaeology*. 2d ed. New York: Biblo and Tannen, 1964.

Burch, Robert. *Simon and the game of chance*. New York: Viking Pr., 1970. Children's book.

Butler, Robert N. *Why survive? Being old in America*. New York: Harper & Row Publishing Co., 1975.

Caine, Lynn. *Widow*. New York: William Morrow & Co., Inc., 1974.
Camps, Frances Ed. and J.M. Cameron. *Practical forensic medicine*. London: Hutchinson Medical Publications, 1956.
Camps, Francis E. ed. *Gradwohl's legal medicine*. Bristol, England: John Wright & Sons, 1968.
Caplan, Gerald. *Principles of preventive psychiatry*. New York: Basic Books Publishing Co., 1964.
Caring for the dying patient and his family; a model for medical education-medical center conferences. New York: Published for the Foundation of Thanatology by Health Sciences Publishing Corp., 1973.
Carlozzi, Carl G. *Death and contemporary man*. Grand Rapids, Michigan: Eerdmans, 1968.
Carlson, Natalie Savage. *The half sisters*. New York: Harper and Row, Publishers, 1970. Children's book.
Carr, Arthur C. et. al. *Grief; selected readings*. New York: Foundation of Thanatology, 1975.
Carrington, Hereward and John R. Meader. *Death, its causes and phenomena*. New York: Dodd, Mead & Co., 1921.
Castelnuovo-Tedesco, P. ed. *Psychiatric aspects of organ transplantation*. New York: Grune & Stratton, Inc., 1971.
Cather, Willa. *Death comes for the archbishop*. New York: Alfred A. Knopf. 1927.
Chadwick, Edwin. *Report . . . on the results of a special inquiry into the practice of interment in towns*. Philadelphia: Printed by C. Sherman, 1845.
Champagne, Marion. *Facing life alone*. Indianapolis: Bobbs-Merrill, 1964.
Chaplin, J. and J. Flynn. *Toward a new life*. Notre Dame, Indiana: Ave Maria Pr., 1971.
Cherescavich, A. *Textbook for nursing assistants*. St. Louis: C.V.Mosby Co., 1964.
Chiles, John R. *A treasury of funeral messages: beauty for ashes*. Grand Rapids, Michigan: Baker Book House, 1960.
Chilson, R. *An introduction to the faith of the Catholics*. New York: Paulist Pr., 1972.
Choron, Jacques. *Death and modern man*. New York: Collier Books, 1964.

Choron, Jacques. *Death and western thought*. New York: Collier Books, 1963.

Choron, Jacques. *Modern man and mortality*. New York: The MacMillan Co., 1963.

Christensen, Halvor N. *Body fluids and their neutrality*. Rev. ed. New York: Oxford University Press, 1963.

Christensen, James L. *The complete funeral manual*. London: Fleming H. Revell Co., 1967.

Claypool, John. *Tracks of a fellow struggler: how to handle grief*. Waco, Texas: Word Books, 1974.

Cleaver, Bill and Vera Cleaver. *Grover*. New York: J.B. Lippincott Co., 1970. Children's book.

Cleaver, Bill and Vera Cleaver. *Where the lilies bloom*. New York: J.B. Lippincott Co., 1969. Children's book.

Coburn, John B. *Anne and the sand dobbies*. New York: Seabury Press, 1964. Children's book.

Cohen, Barbara. *Thank you, Jackie Robinson*. New York: Lothrop, Lee and Shepard, 1974. Children's book.

Cohen, Daniel. *The body snatchers*. Philadelphia, Pennsylvania: J.B. Lippincott Co., 1975.

Compton, W.H. *Funeral sermon outlines*. Grand Rapids, Michigan: Baker Book House, 1965.

Conference on Identifying Suicide Potential. Teachers College, Columbia University, 1969. *Identifying suicide potential; conference proceedings.*. Edited by Dorothy B. Anderson and Lenora J. McClean. New York: Behavioral Publication, 1971.

Cook, Sarah et. al. *Children and dying; an exploration and a selective professional bibliography.* New York: Health Science Publishing Corp., 1973.

Coriolis. *Death, here is thy sting*. Toronto: McClelland and Stewart Publishers, 1967.

Corley, Elizabeth A. *Tell me about death, tell me about funerals*. Santa Clara, California: Grammatical Sciences, 1973. Children's book.

Coutant, Helen. *First snow*. New York: Alfred A. Knopf, 1974.

Crane, Diana. *Social aspects of the prolongation of life. (Social Science Frontiers*, v. 1). New York: Russell Sage Foundation, 1969.

Crane, Stephen, *Red badge of courage*. New York: Random House, 1951.

Craven, Margaret. *I heard the owl call my name*. Garden City, New York: Doubleday and Co., 1973.

Cummings, E. and W. Henry. *Growing old*. New York: Basic Books, 1961.

Curran, William J. and E. Donald Shapiro. *Law, medicine and forensic science*. Boston: Little, Brown and Co., 1970.

Curry, Alan S. *Poison detection in human organs*. Springfield, Illinois: Charles C. Thomas, 1963.

Curtin, Sharon R. *Nobody ever died of old age*. Boston: Little, Brown & Co., 1973.

Cutolo, S.R. *Bellevue is my home*. Garden City: Doubleday & Co., Inc., 1956.

Cutler, D.R. ed. *Updating life and death: essays in ethics and medicine*. Boston: Beacon Pr., 1969.

Dastre, A. *Life and death* translated by W.I. Greenstreet. London: W. Scott, 1911.

David, Daniel L. *What to do when death comes*. New York: Federation of Reform Temples.

David, R.H. ed. *Dealing with death*. Los Angeles: Andrus Gerontology Center, University of Southern California, 1973.

Davidson, Glen W. *Living with dying*. Minneapolis, Minnesota: Augsburg Publishing House, 1975.

Davies, Maurice R.R. *The law of burial: cremation and exhumation*. 2d ed. London: Shaw and Sons, 1966.

Davis, Fred. *Passage through crisis*. Indianapolis: Bobbs-Merrill, 1964.

Deacy, William H. *Memorials today for tomorrow*. Tate, Georgia: Georgia Marble Co., 1928.

Death education: preparation for living. Cambridge: Schenkman Publishing Co., 1971.

Death in early America: history, customs, superstitions and folklore. Nashville, Tennessee: Thomas Nelson, Inc., 1976.

Decker, Beatrice and Gladys Kooiman. *After the flowers have gone*. Grand Rapids, Michigan: Zondervan Publishing House, 1973.

Dempsey, David. *The way we die*. New York: MacMillan and Co., 1975.

DePaola, Tomie. *Nana upstairs and Nana downstairs*. New York: G.P. Putnam's Sons, 1973. Children's book.

Deutsch, Felix ed. *The psychosomatic concepts in psychoanalysis*. New York: International Universities Pr., 1953.

DeVries, Peter. *The blood of the Lamb*. Boston: Little, Brown & Co., 1961.

Didier, Jean-Charles. *Death and the Christian*. New York: Hawthorn Books, Inc., 1961.

Dobrin, Arnold. *Scat*! Englewood Cliffs, New Jersey: Scholastic Book Services, 1973. Children's book.

Dr. X. *Intern*. New York: Harper & Row Publishers, 1956.

Donne, John. *Deaths duell, or a consolation to the soule against the dying life*. Facsimile ed. New York: Scholar Pr., 1631.

Dooley, Thomas A. *Doctor Tom Dooley, my story*. New York: Farrar, Strauss, and Co., 1960.

Dorozynski, A. *The man they wouldn't let die*. New York: The MacMillan Co., 1956.

Douglass, William A. *Death in Murelaga; funerary ritual in a Spanish Basque village*. Seattle, Washington: University of Washington Press, c1969.

Downing, A.B. ed. *Euthanasia and the right to death*. New York: Humanities Pr., 1971.

Draper, Edgar. *Psychiatry and pastoral care*. Englewood Cliffs, New Jersey: Prentice-Hall, Inc., 1965.

Draznin, Yaffa. *How to prepare for death: your own or someone else's*. New York: Hawthorn Books, Inc., 1976.

Dublin, Louis I. *Suicide: a sociological and statistical study*. New York: Ronald Pr., 1963.

Ducasse, C.J. *Nature, Mind and Death*. LaSalle, Illinois: Open Court Publishing Co., 1951.

Ducasse, Curt John. *A critical examination of the belief in a life after death*. Springfield, Illinois: C.C. Thomas Co., 1961.

Dumont, Richard G. and Dennis C. Foss. *The American view of death: acceptance or denial*? Cambridge, Massachusetts: Schenkman Publishing Co., Inc., 1972.

Dunne, John S. *The city of the Gods; a study in myth and mortality*. New York: MacMillan, 1965.

Durkheim, Emile. *Suicide: a study in sociology*. Glencoe, Illinois: Free Pr., 1951.

Edman, V. Raymond. *But God*! Grand Rapids, Michigan: Zondervan Publishing House, 1969.

Eissler, K.R. *The psychiatrist and the dying patient*. New York: International Universities Press, 1955.

Ellis, E.R. and G.N. Allen. *Within our suicide problem*. Garden City: New York: Doubleday, 1961.

Eminyan, Maurice. *The theology of salvation*. Boston: Daughters of St. Paul, 1960.

Epstein, Charlotte. *Nursing the dying patient*. Reston, Virginia: Reston Publishing Co., Inc., 1975.

Erdman, Lolla Grace. *A bluebird will do*. New York: Dodd, Mead and Co., 1973. Children's book.

Erlich, P.R. *The population bomb*. New York: Ballantine Books, Inc., 1968.

Ettinger, Robert C.W. *Prospect of immortality*. 1st ed. Garden City, New York: Doubleday 1964.

Euthanasia and the right to death. New York: Humanities Press, 1970.

Evans, Jocelyn. *Living with a man who is dying*. New York: Taplinger Publishing Co., 1971.

Evans, William E.D. *The chemistry of death*. Springfield, Illinois: C.C. Thomas Co., 1963.

Farber, Maurice L. *Theory of suicide*. New York: Funk and Wagnalls, 1968.

Farberow, N.L. and E.S. Shneidman ed. *The cry for help*. New York: McGraw-Hill, 1961.

Farberow, Norman L. ed. *Taboo topics*. New York: Atherton Press, 1963.

Fargues, Marie. *The child and the mystery of death*. Glenn Rock, New Jersey: Dews Books, 1966.

Farley, Carolyn, *The garden is doing fine*. New York: Atheneum, 1975. Children's book.

Fassler, Joan. *My Grandpa died today*. New York: Human Sciences Press, Division of Behavioral Publications, Inc., 1971.

Feifel, Herman ed. *The meaning of death*. New York: McGraw-Hill Book Co., 1959.

Feinstein, Alvan R. *Clinical judgment*. Baltimore: Williams & Wilkins Co., 1967.

Fenichel, Otto. *The psychoanalytic theory of neurosis*. New York: W.W. Norton & Co., 1967.

Fiedler, Leslie A. *Love and death in the American novel*. New York: Criterion Books, 1960.

Field, M. *Patients are people*. New York: Columbia University Pr., 1953.

Fitzhugh, Louise and Sandra Scoppettone. *Bang, bang, you're dead*. New York: Harper & Row, 1969. Children's book.

Fletcher, Joseph. *Morals and medicine*. Boston: Beacon Pr., 1960.

Flew, Anthony ed. *Body, mind and death*. New York: MacMillan Publishing Co., Inc., 1964.

Ford, William H. *Simple sermons for funeral services*. Grand Rapids, Michigan: Zondervan, 1962.

Foss, Martin. *Death, sacrifice and tragedy*. Lincoln, Nebraska: University of Nebraska Press, 1966.

Fox, R. *Experiment perilous*. New York: Free Pr., 1963.

Frank, Anne. *The diary of a young girl*. New York: Washington Square Press, 1963.

Frankl, Viktor E. *From death camp to existentialism: a psychiatrist's path to a new therapy* Boston: Beacon Pr., 1959.

Frazer, James G. *The belief in immortality and the worship of the dead*. London: MacMillan and Co., 1913.

Frazer, Sir James G. *The fear of the dead in primitive religion*. New York: Biblo and Tannen, 1966.

Freeman, L. *Hospital in action: the story of Michael Reese Medical Center*. Skokie, Illinois: Rand McNally & Co., 1956.

Fremantle, F. and C. Trungpa tr. *The Tibetan book of the dead.* New York: Shambala Pubs., c/o Random House, 1975.

Frenkl, V.E. *The doctor and soul*. New York: Alfred A. Knopf, Inc., 1955.

Freud, Anna and D.T. Burlinham. *Infants without families*. New York: International University Press, 1944.

Freud, S. *Civilization and its discontents*. London: Hogarth Pr., 1933.

Freud, S. *Mourning and melancholia*. London: Hogarth Pr., 1957.

Freud, S. *Totem and taboo*. New York: W.W. Norton & Co., Inc., 1952.

Freud, Sigmund. *Civilization, war and death; selections from five works*. London: The Hogarth Press and the Institute of Psychoanalysis, 1953.

Fridland, L. *The achievement of Soviet medicine*. New York: Twayne Publishers, Inc., 1961.

Friedman, Paul. *On suicide*. New York: International Universities Pr., 1967.

Fromm, Erich. *Escape from freedom*. New York: Henry Holt & Co., 1941.

Fromm, Erich. *Man for himself*. New York: Henry Holt & Co., 1947.

Fulton, Robert. *A compilation of studies of attitudes towards death, funerals and funeral directors*. Minneapolis: University of Minnesota, Center for Death Education, 1971.

Fulton, Robert. *Death and identity*. New York: John Wiley and Sons, Inc., 1965.

Fulton, Robert comp. *Death, grief and bereavement: a bibliography, 1845-1975*. New York: Arno Pr., 1976.

Fulton, Robert. *The sacred and the secular: attitudes of the American public toward death*. Milwaukee: Bulfin Printers, 1963.

Funeral service facts and figures. n.p. 1959 - . Annual publication.

Furman, Erna. *A child's parent dies*. New Haven, Connecticut: Yale University Press, 1974.

Furman, R. *Loss and grief; the child's reaction to a death in the family*. New York: Columbia University Pr., 1970.

Gaevskoia, Maria S. *Biochemistry of the brain during the process of dying and resuscitation*. New York: Consultants Bureau, 1964.

Gale, Frederick C. *Mortuary science*. Springfield, Illinois: C.C. Thomas Co., 1961.

Garner, H.H. *Psychosomatic management of the patient with malignancy*. Springfield, Illinois: Charles C. Thomas, 1966.

Garrigou-Lagrange, R. *Life everlasting*. St. Louis: B. Herder Book Co., 1952.

Gatch, Milton. *Death; meaning and mortality in Christian thought and contemporary culture*. New York: Seabury Press, 1969.

Gavey, C. *The management of the "hopeless" case*. London: H.K. Lewis, 1952.

Gebhart, J.C. *Funeral costs*. New York: Putnam, 1928.

George, Jean Craighead. *Julia of the wolves*. New York: Harper and Row Publishers, 1972.

Gibbs, Jack P. comp. *Suicide*. New York: Harper, 1968.

Giesey, Ralph E. *The royal funeral ceremony in renaissance France*. Geneva Switzerland: E. Droz, 1960.

Gillon, E.V., Jr. *Victorian cemetery art*. New York: Dover Publications, Inc., 1972.

Gittelsohn, Roland B. *Man's best hope*. New York: Random House, 1961.

Glaser, Barney and Strauss, Anselm L. *Awareness of Dying*. Chicago: Aldine Publishing Co., 1965.

Glaser, Barney G. *Time for dying*. Chicago: Aldine, 1968.

Glasser, Ronald J. *Ward four hundred two*. New York: George Braziller, Inc., 1973.

Glick, Ira O., Robert Weiss, and C.M. Markes. *The first year of bereavement*. New York: John Wiley & Sons, 1974.

Godin, Andre. *Death and presence: the psychology of death and afterlife*. Brussels: Lumen Vitae Pr., 1972.

Goffman, E. *Stigma*. Englewood Cliffs, N.J.: Prentice-Hall, Inc., 1963.

Gonzales, Thomas A. *Legal medicine: pathology and toxicology*. 2d ed. New York: Appleton, c1954.

Goodrich, Robert E. *On the other side of sorrow*. Nashville, Tennessee: Abingdon, 1962.

Goody, John R. *Death, property and the ancestors; a study of the mortuary customs of the La Dogoa of West Africa*. Stanford, California: Stanford University Press, 1962.

Gordon, Albert I. *In times of sorrow*. New York: United Synagogues of America, 1949.

Gordon, David Cole. *Overcoming the fear of death*. Baltimore, Maryland: Penguin Books, Inc., 1972.

Gorer, Geoffrey. *Death, grief and mourning: a study of contemporary society*. Garden City, New York: Doubleday Publishing Co., 1967.

Gorer, G. *Death, grief and mourning in contemporary Britain*. London: Cresset, 1965.

Govern, Elaine. *Ice cream next summer*. Chicago: Albert Whitman, 1973. Children's book.

Gray, Thomas. *An elegy wrote in a country church yard*. Facsimile edition. New York: Scholar Pr., 1751.

Green, Betty R. and Donald Irish. *Death education: preparation for living* Cambridge, Massachusetts: Schenkman Publishing Co., 1971.

Greenberg, Bradley S. and Edwin R. Parker ed. *The Kennedy assassination and the American public: social communication in crisis*. Stanford, California: Stanford University Pr., 1965.

Greenberg, Sidney. *A modern treasury of Jewish thoughts*. New York: Thomas Yoseloff, 1960.

Grollman, Earl A. ed. *Concerning death: a practical guide for the living*. Boston, Massachusetts: Beacon Press, 1974.

Grollman, Earl A. ed. *Explaining death to children*. Boston: Beacon Pr., 1969.

Grollman, Earl A. *Judaism in Sigmund Freud's world*. New York: Appleton-Century-Crofts, 1966.

Grollman, Earl A. *Rabbinical counseling*. New York: Bloch, 1967.

Grollman, Earl A. *Suicide: prevention, intervention, postvention*. Boston: Beacon Pr., 1971.

Grollman, Earl A. ed. *Talking about death: a dialog between parent and child*. Boston: Beacon Press, 1970.

Gruman, Gerald J. *A history of ideas about the prolongation of life; the evolution of prolongevity hypothesis to 1800*. Philadephia: American Philosophical Society, 1966.

Gunther, John. *Death be not proud*. New York: Harper & Row, Inc., 1949.

Gutzke, Manford G. *Fear not: a Christian view of death*. Grand Rapids, Michigan: Baker Book House, 1974.

Habenstein, Robert Wesley and William M. Lamers. *Funeral customs the world over*. Milwaukee: Bulfin Printers, 1963.

Habenstein, Robert Wesley and William M. Lamers. *The history of American funeral directing*. Milwaukee: Bulfin Printers, 1955.

Hafen, Brent Q. and Eugen J. Faux ed. *Self-destructive behavior: a national crisis*. Minneapolis, Minnesota: Burgess Publishing Co., 1972.

Haim, Andre. *Adolescent suicide*. New York: International Universities Pr., 1974.

Hamovitch, Maurice B. *The parent and the fatally ill child*. Los Angeles: Delman Publishing Co., 1964.

Handke, Peter. *A sorrow beyond dreams, a life story*. New York: Farrar, Strauss and Giroux, 1974.

Harmer, B. *Textbook of the principles and practice of nursing*. 5th ed. New York: The MacMillan Co., 1955.

Harmer, Ruth M. *The high cost of dying*. New York: Crowell-Collier, 1963.

Harmon, Nolan B. ed. *The pastor's ideal funeral manual*. Nashville, Tennessee: Abingdon Pr., 1970.

Harrington, Alan. *The immortalist; an approach to the engineering of man's divinity*. New York: Random House, 1969.

Harris, Audrey. *Why did he die?* Minneapolis, Minnesota: Lerner Publications Co., 1965.

Harris, Raymond I. *Outline of death investigation*. Springfield, Illinois: C.C. Thomas, 1962.

Havner, Vance. *Though I walk through the valley*. Old Tappan, New Jersey: Fleming J. Revell Co., 1974.

Heidel, Alexander. *The Gilgamesh Epic and Old Testament parallels*. 2d ed. Chicago: University of Chicago Press, 1949.

Hemingway, Ernest. *A farewell to arms*. New York: Charles Scribner's Sons, 1929.

Henderson, Joseph L. *The wisdom of the serpent; the myths of death, rebirth and resurrection*. New York: G. Braziller, 1963.

Hendin, David. *Death as a fact of life*. New York: W.W. Norton & Co., 1973.

Hendin, David. *Death as a Fact of Life*. New York: Warner Books, Inc., 1974.

Henry, Andrew F. and James F. Short, Jr. *Suicide and homicide*. Glencoe, Illinois: Free Pr., 1954.

Hertzberg, Arthur ed. *Judaism*. New York: Washington Square Pr., 1963.

Herzog, Edgar. *Psyche and death*. New York: G.P. Putnam & Sons, 1972.

Hetzler, Florence. *Death and creativity; an interdisciplinary encounter*. New York: Health Sciences Pub. Corp., 1976.

Hetzler, Florence M., J. Carse and A.H. Kutscher. *Philosophical concepts of death; essays on thanatology*. New York: Foundation of Thanatology, 1976.

Hick, John. *Death and eternal life*. London: Collins, 1976.

Hickey, Tom. *Grief: its recognition and resolution*. University Park Press, Pennsylvania State University, 1973.

Hinton, John. *Dying*. Baltimore, MD: Penguin Books Inc., 1972.

Hocking, William E. *The meaning of immortality in human experience, including thoughts on death and life*. Rev. ed. New York: Harper, 1957.

Hoffman, Dona. *Yes, Lord.* St. Louis, Missouri: Concordia Publishing House, 1975.

Hoffman, Frederick J. *The mortal no: death and the modern imagination.* Princeton, New Jersey: Princeton University Press, 1964.

Hoffman, Joseph G. *The life and death of cells.* Garden City, New York Doubleday, 1957.

Holck, Frederick H. ed. *Death and Eastern thought.* Nashville, Tennessee: Abingdon Press, 1974.

The Holy Scriptures. Philadelphia: The Jewish Publication Society of America, 1917.

Houts, Marshall. *Where death delights; the story of Dr. Milton Halpern and forensic medicine.* New York: Coward-McCann, 1967.

Hsu, Francis L.K. *Under the ancestor's shadow; Chinese culture and personality.* New York: Columbia University Press, 1948.

Hunnisett, R.F. *The medieval coroner.* London: Cambridge University Press, 1961.

Hunt, Gladys. *The Christian way of death.* Grand Rapids, Michigan: Zondervan Publishing House, 1971.

Hunt, Gladys. *Don't be afraid to die.* Grand Rapids, Michigan: Zondervan Publishing House, 1974.

Hunt, Irene. *Across five Aprils.* Chicago: Follett, 1964. Children's book.

Hutton, Samuel W. *Minister' funeral manual.* Grand Rapids, Michigan: Baker Book House, 1968.

Irion, Paul E. *Cremation.* Philadelphia: Fortress Press, 1968.

Irion, Paul E. *The funeral and the mourner.* New York: Abingdon Press, 1954.

Irion, Paul E. *The funeral - vestige or value?* New York: Abingdon Press, 1966.

Isham, Lorraine S. *Survey of state laws governing the disposal of the dead and regulating those who work with the dead: a critical look at the laws.* Hanover, New Hampshire: Billings Lee, 1966.

Jackson, Edgar. *You and your grief.* New York: Channel Press, c1962.

Jackson, Edgar N. *Telling a child about death.* New York: Channel Press, 1965.

Jackson, Edgar N. *Understanding grief*. New York: Abingdon Press, 1957.

Jackson, Edgar N. *When someone dies*. Philadelphia: Fortress Press, 1971.

Jackson, Edgar Newman. *The Christian funeral; its meaning, its purpose, and its modern practice*. 1st ed. New York: Channel Press, 1966.

Jackson, Edgar Newman. *For the living*. Des Moines: Channell Press, 1964.

Jacobs, C. Walker. *Stranger, stop and cast an eye; a guide to gravestones and rubbings*. Brattleboro, Vermont: Stephen Greene Pr., 1973.

Jakobovits, I. *Jewish medical ethics*. New York: Bloch Publishing Co., 1967.

Johnson, Mildred. *The smiles and the tears*. Old Tappan, New Jersey: Fleming Revell, 1969.

Jonas, Hans. *The phenomenon of life*. New York: Harper and Row, Inc., 1966.

Jones, Barbara M. *Design for death*. Indianapolis: Bobbs-Merrill, 1967.

Jones, P. Herbert ed. *Cremation in Great Britain*. 3d ed. London: Thaws Pr., 1945.

Jones, William Tudor. *Metaphysics of life and death*. New York: George H. Doran Co., 1924.

Jordahl, Edna K. *Helping Children Understand Death*. St. Paul: University of Minnesota Agricultural Extension Service, 1968.

Joseph, Stephen. *Children in fear*. New York: Holt, Rinehart and Winston, 1974.

Journal of Clinical Child Psychology III, No. 2, Summer 1974 (the entire issue is on death and children).

Kalish, R.A. *Death and bereavement: an annotated social science bibliography*. Private circulation, 1964.

Kalish, R.A. *Supplement to bibliography on death and breavement*. Private circulation, 1965.

Kantrowitz, Adrian et al. *Who shall live and who shall die; the ethical implications of the New Medical Technology*. New York: Union of American Hebrew Congresses, 1968.

Kantorowitz, Mildred. *When Violet died*. New York: Parent's Magazine Press, 1973. Children's book.

Kapleau, Philip ed. *The wheel of death*. New York: Harper & Row, Publishers, 1971.

Kastenbaum, Robert and Ruth Aisenberg. *The psychology of death*. New York: Springer Publishing Co., Inc., 1972.

Kavanaugh, Robert E. *Facing death*. Baltimore: Penguin Books, Inc., 1972.

Keleman, Stanley. *Living your dying*. New York: Random House, 1974.

Kelly, Orville E. *Make today count*. New York: Delacorte Pr., 1975.

Kierkegaard, Soren. *Fear and trembling - the sickness unto death*. Garden City, New York: Doubleday & Co., Inc., 1954.

Kipling, Rudyard. *The jungle book*. Garden City, New York: Doubleday, 1964. Children's book.

Klagsbrun, Francine. *Too young to die*. New York: Houghton-Mifflin, 1976.

Klein, Norma. *Sunshine*. New York: Avon, 1974.

Klein, Stanley. *The final mystery*. Garden City, New York: Doubleday & Co., Inc., 1974.

Kliman, G.K. *Psychological emergencies of childhood*. New York: Grune and Stratton, 1968.

Kluge, Eike-Henrer W. *The practice of death*. New Haven, Connecticut: Yale Univ. Pr., 1975.

Klupar, G.J. *Modern cemetery management*. Archdiocese of Chicago: Catholic Cemeteries, 1962.

Koch, Ron. *Goodbye Grandpa*. Minneapolis, Minnesota: Augsburg Publishing House, 1975.

Koestenbaum, Peter. *Is there an answer to death?* Englewood Cliffs, New Jersey: Prentice-Hall, Inc., 1976.

Kooiman, Gladys. *When death takes a father*. Grand Rapids, Michigan: Baker Book House, 1968.

Kreis, Bernadine. *Up from grief; patterns of recovery*. New York: Seabury Press, 1969.

Krieger, Wilber M. *A complete guide to funeral service management*. Englewood Cliffs, New Jersey: Prentice-Hall, 1962.

Kubler-Ross, Elisabeth. *Death: the final stage of growth*. Englewood Cliffs, New Jersey: Prentice-Hall, Inc., 1975.

Kubler-Ross, E. *Images of growth and death*. Englewood Cliffs, New Jersey: Prentice-Hall, 1976.

Kubler-Ross, Elisabeth. *On death and dying.* New York: The MacMillan Co., 1973.

Kubler-Ross, Elisabeth. *Questions and answers on death and dying.* New York: Collier Books, a Division of MacMillan Publishing Co., Inc., 1974.

Kull, Andrew. *New England cemeteries.* Brattleboro, Vermont: Stephen Greene Pr., 1975.

Kurz, Albert L. *Beyond discouragement.* New York: Vantage, 1969.

Kutscher, Austin H. *But not to loose; a book of comfort for those bereaved.* New York: F. Fell, 1969.

Kutscher, Austin H. *Death and bereavement.* Springfield, Illinois: C.C. Thomas Co., 1969.

Kutscher, Austin H. *A comprehensive bibliography of the thanatology literature.* New York: MSS Information Corp., 1975.

Kutscher, Austin H. and Austin H. Kutscher, Jr. *Bibliography of books on death, bereavement, loss and grief, 1935-1968.* New York: Health Sciences Publishing Corp., 1969. Supplement I, 1968-1972. 1974.

Kutscher, Austin H. and Lilian G. ed. *Religion and bereavement.* New York: Health Sciences Pub. Corp., 1972.

Kutscher, Austin H. Jr. and Lillian G. Kutscher. *For the bereaved.* New York: F. Fell, 1971.

Kutscher, Austin H. and M.R. Goldberg ed. *Caring for the dying patient and his family.* New York: Health Sciences Pub. Corp., 1973.

Laas, William. *Monuments in your history.* New York: Popular Library, 1972.

Lamers, William, Jr. *Death, grief, mourning the funeral and the child.* Chicago: National Association of Funeral Directors, November 1, 1965.

Lamm, Norman. *The Jewish way in death and mourning.* New York: Jonathan David Publishers, 1969.

Lamont, Corliss. *A humanist funeral service.* Yellow Springs, Ohio: American Humanist Association, 1954.

Lamont, Corliss. *The illusion of immortality.* 4th ed. New York: F. Ungar Pub. Co., 1965.

Landorf, Joyce. *Mourning song.* Old Tappan, New Jersey: Fleming H. Revell Co., 1974.

Langer, Mario. *Learning to live as a widow*. New York: Julian Messner, 1957.
Langone, John. *Death is a noun*. New York: Dell Publishing Co., Inc., 1972.
Lasagna, Louis. *The doctors' dilemmas*. New York: Harper, 1962.
Lazarus, O. *Liberal Judaism and its standpoint*. London: MacMillan, 1937.
Lee, Reuel P. *Burial customs, ancient and modern*. Minneapolis: The Arya Co., 1929.
Lee, Virginia. *The magic moth*. New York: Seabury Press, 1974.
L'Engle, Madeleine. *Meet the Austins*. New York: The Vanguard Press, 1960. Children's book.
L'Engle, Madeleine. *A wrinkle in time*. New York: Farrar, Strauss, and Giroux, 1962. Children's book.
Leogrande, Ernie. *A second chance to live*. New York: Da Capo, 1976.
Lepp, Ignace. *Death and its mysteries*. New York: MacMillan, 1968.
Lerner, E. and I. Lerner comp. *Devils, demons, death and damnation*. New York: Dover Publications, Inc., 1971.
Levit, Rose. *Ellen: a short life long remembered*. San Francisco: Chronicle Books, 1974.
Lewis, C.S. *A Grief observed*. New York: Seabury Press, 1961.
Lewis, Oscar. *A death in the Sanchez family*. New York: Random House, 1969.
Liebman, Joshua L. *Peace of mind*. New York: Simon & Schuster, 1946.
Lifton, Robert J. *Challenges of humanistic psychology*, edited by James F.T. Bugental. New York: McGraw-Hill Book Co., 1967.
Lifton, Robert Jay and Eric Olson. *Living and dying*. New York: Praeger Publishers, 1974.
Litzinger, John C. *Know your mortician: an inside view of the funeral profession*. New York: Exposition Press, 1963.
Lockyer, Herbert. *The funeral sourcebook*. Grand Rapids, Michigan: Zondervan, 1967.
Loether, Herman J. *Problems of aging: sociological and social psychological perspectives*. Belmont, California: Dickenson Publishing Co., Inc., 1967.
Long, Samuel Burman. *Be ye comforted*. Boston: Meador Pub. Co., 1944.

Lopata, Helena Z. *Widowhood in an American city*. Cambridge, Massachusetts: Schenkman Publishing Co., 1973.

Lopatin, I.A. *The cult of the dead among the natives of the Amur Basin*. The Hague: Mouton and Co., 1960.

The Lord is my Shepherd - a book of wake services. Notre Dame, Indiana: Ave Maria Pr., 1971.

Lorenzo, Carol Lee. *Mama's ghosts*. New York: Harper and Row Publishers, 1974. Children's book.

Lund, Doris. *Eric*. Philadelphia, Pennsylvania: J.B. Lippincott Co., 1974.

McConkey, Clarence. *When cancer comes*. Philadelphia: The Westminster Press, 1974.

McCoy, Marjorie Casebier. *To die with style*. Nashville, Tennessee: Abingdon Pr., 1974.

MacEachern, M. *Hospital organization and management*, 3d ed. Chicago: Physicians Record Co., 1957.

McHugh, James T. *Death, dying and the law*. Huntington, Indiana: Our Sunday Visitor, Inc. and Bishops' Committee for Pro-life Activities, National Conference of Catholic Bishops, 1976.

Mack, Adrien ed. *Death in American experience*. New York: Schocken Books, 1973.

McLarry, Newman R. *When shadows fall*. Nashville, Tennessee: Broadman Press, 1960.

Madden, Myron C. *Raise the dead*. Waco, Texas: Word Books, 1975.

Maeterlinch, Maurice. *Our eternity*. London: Methuen & Co., Ltd., 1913.

Mailer, N. *The naked and the dead*. New York: Signet Books, 1958.

Maguire, Daniel C. *Death by choice*. New York: Schocken Books, 1973.

Manchester, William. *The death of a president November 20-November 25, 1963*. New York: Harper and Row, Inc., 1967.

Mann, Thomas C. and Janet Greene. *Over their dead bodies: Yankee epitaphs and history*. Brattleboro, Vermont: Greene Press, 1962.

Mann, Thomas C. and J. Greene. *Sudden and awful; American epitaphs and the finger of God*. Brattleboro, Vermont: Stephen Greene Pr., 1968.

Mannes, Marya. *Last Rights*. New York: William Morrow & Co., Inc., 1974.

Marks, Elaine. *Simone de Beauvoir: encounters with death*. New Brunswick, New Jersey: Rutgers University Pr., 1973.

Marks, Renee U. *The sociology of death: a selected bibliography*. Ann Arbor, Michigan: University of Michigan, School of Public Health, Department of Epidemiology, 1965.

Marris, P. *Widows and their families*. London: Routledge and Kegan Paul, 1958.

Marris, Peter. *Loss and change*. New York: Random House, 1974.

Marshall, Catherine. *Beyond ourselves*. New York: McGraw-Hill, 1961.

Marshall, Catherine. *To live again*. New York: McGraw-Hill, 1957.

Martin, Edward A. *Psychology of funeral service*. 4th ed. Springfield, Ohio: Champion, 1962.

Martin, Patricia M. *John Fitzgerald Kennedy*. New York: G.P. Putnam's Sons, 1964. Children's book.

Matson, Archie. *The waiting world: what happens after death*. New York: Harper and Row Publishers, 1975.

Maxwell, Edith. *Just dial a number*. New York: Dodd, Mead and Co., 1971.

Mazer, Norma Fox. *A figure of speech*. New York: Delacorte Pr., 1973. Children's book.

Meer, Fatima. *Race and suicide in South Africa*. Boston, Massachusetts: Routledge and Kegan Paul, 1976.

Meerloo, Joost A. *Suicide and mass suicide*. New York: Grune and Stratton, 1962.

Mendenhall, G.E. *Law and covenant in Israel and the ancient Near East*. Pittsburgh: Biblical Colloquium, 1955.

Menninger, Karl. *Man against himself*. New York: Harcourt, Brace & Co., 1938.

Merkeley, Donald K. *The investigation of death*. Springfield, Illinois: C.C. Thomas Co., 1957.

Mersch, Emile. *Morality and the mystical body*. New York: P.J. Kenedy & Sons, 1939.

Merton, R.K., G. Reader, and P. Kendall ed. *The student physician*. Cambridge: Harvard University Pr., 1957.

Meyer, Joachim E. *Death and neurosis*. New York: International University Pr., Inc., 1975.

Miles, Miska. *Annie and the old one*. Boston: Little, Brown and Co., 1971. Children's book.

Miller, Arthur. *Death of a salesman*. New York: The Viking Pr., 1949.

Mills, Listor ed. *Perspectives on death*. Nashville, Tennessee: Abingdon Press, 1969.

Mills, Gretchen C., Raymond Reisler, et al. *Discussing death; a guide to death education*. Homewood, Illinois: ETC Publications, 1975.

Mishima, Yukio. *Death in midsummer and other stories*. New York: New Directions Book, 1966.

Mishima, Yukio. *Runaway horses*. New York: Alfred A Knopf, 1973.

Mishima, Yukio. *Sun and steel*, translated by John Bester. New York: Grove Press, 1970.

Mitchell, Marjorie E. *The child's attitude to death*. New York: Schocken Books, 1967.

Mitford, Jessica. *The American way of death*. New York: Simon and Schuster, 1963.

Mitscherlich, Alexander and Margarete. *Inability to mourn*. New York: Random House, 1975.

Mohr, G.J. *When children face crises*. Chicago: Spencer Pr., Inc., 1952.

Mohr, Nicholasa. *El Bronx remembered*. New York: Harper and Row Publishers, 1975.

Mohr, Nicholasa. *Nilda*. New York: Harper and Row, 1973.

Moody, Anne. *Mr. death: four stories*. New York: Harper and Row Publishers, 1975.

Moore, Clifford H. *Ancient beliefs in the immortality of the soul, with some account of their influence on later views*. New York: Cooper Square Publishers, 1963.

Moore, F.D. *Give and take: the development of tissue transplantation*. Philadelphia: Saunders, 1964.

Moore, F.D. *Transplant: the give and take of tissue transplantation*. New York: Simon and Schuster, 1972.

Moore, George Foote. *Judaism*. Cambridge: Harvard University Pr., 1946.

Morgan, Ernest ed. *A manual of death education and simple burial*. Burnsville, North Carolina: The Celo Press, 1975.

Moriarty, David M. *The loss of loved ones; the effects of a death in the family on personality development.* Springfield, Illinois: C.C. Thomas Co., 1957.

Mortuary caretaker. Arco Publishing Co., Inc., 1965.

Motto, Jerome et. al. ed. *Standards for suicide prevention and crisis centers.* New York: Human Sciences Pr., 1974.

Muggeridge, Malcolm. *Something beautiful for God.* New York: Ballentine Books, Inc., 1973.

Mumford, Lewis. *Green memories.* New York: Harcourt, Brace and World, 1947.

Munnichs, J.M.A. *Old age and finitude; a contribution to psychogerontology.* Basil: S. Karger, 1966.

Myers, Frederic W.H. *Human personality and its survival after death.* New Hyde Park, New York: University Books, 1961.

Nagy, Maria H. *The meaning of death.* New York: McGraw-Hill Publishing Co., 1965.

Neale, Robert E. *The art of dying.* New York: Harper & Row, Publishers, 1973.

Negovskii, V.A. *Resuscitation and artificial hypothermia.* New York: Consultants Bureau Enterprises, Inc., 1962.

Nelson, James B. *Human medicine: ethical perspectives on new medical issues.* Minneapolis, Minnesota: Augsburg Publishing House, 1973.

Newman, Joseph ed. *Teach your wife how to be a widow.* Washington, D.C.: U.S. News and World Report, 1973. For sale by Simon and Schuster.

Niebuhr, H.R. *The responsible self.* New York: Harper & Row., 1963.

Nobel Conference, 8th. Gustavus Adolphus College, 1972. *The end of life.* A discussion at the Nobel Conference, organized by Gustavus Adolphus College, St. Peter, Minnesota, 1972. Ansterdam: North-Holland Publishing Co., 1973.

Nowell, R. *What a modern Catholic believes about death.* Chicago: Thomas More Pr., 1972.

Oates, Wayne E. and Kirk H. Neely. *Where to go for help.* Philadelphia: Westminster Pr., 1972.

Ochs, Robert. *The death in every now.* New York: Sheed & Ward, Inc., 1969.

O'Connor, Sr. M. Catherine. *The art of dying well.* New York: AMS Press, Inc., 1942, 1974.

Ostheimer, Nancy C. and J.M. *Life or death; who controls.* New York: Springer Publishing Co., 1976.

Owen, J.K. *Modern concepts of hospital administration.* Philadelphia: W.B. Saunders, 1962.

Palmer, Charles E. *Religions and rehabilitation.* Springfield, Illinois: C.C. Thomas Co., 1968.

Noveck, Simon. *Judaism and psychiatry.* New York: United Synagogues of America, 1956.

Panofsky, Erwin. *Tomb sculpture; four lectures on its changing aspects from ancient Egypt to Bernini.* New York: H.N. Abrams, 1964.

Parkes, Colin Murray. *Bereavement: studies of grief in adult life.* New York: International Universities Press, Inc., 1972.

Parrinder, Jeoffrey. *Something after death?* Niles, Illinois: Argus Communications, 1970.

Parrott, Leslie. *The usher's manual: a spiritual and practical guidebook.* Grand Rapids, Michigan: Zondervan, 1970.

Paton, Lewis Bayles. *Spiritism and the cult of the dead in antiquity.* New York: MacMillan, 1921.

Peale, Norman Vincent. *The healing of sorrow.* New York: Doubleday, 1966.

Pearl, R. *The biology of death.* Philadelphia: J.B. Lippincott Co., 1922.

Pearson, Leonard ed. *Death and dying: current issues in the treatment of the dying person.* Cleveland, Ohio: The Press of Case Western Reserve University, 1969.

Peck, H.B. *Extending and developing manpower for urban community mental health centers.* New York: Lincoln Hospital Health Services, 1964.

Peck, Robert Newton. *A day no pigs would die.* New York: Dell, 1972.

Pelikan, Jaroslav. *The shape of death, life, death and immortality in the early fathers.* New York: Abingdon Pr., 1961.

Philipon, M.M. *The sacraments in the Christian life.* Westminster, Maryland: Newman Pr., 1953.

Phipps, Joyce. *Death's single privacy.* New York: Seabury Press, 1974.

Picard, Barbara L. *Stories of King Arthur and his knights*. New York: Oxford Press, 1955.

Pieper, J. *Death and immortality*. New York: Herder and Herder, 1969.

Pincus, Lily. *Death and the family: the family: the importance of mourning*. New York: Vintage Books, 1974.

Pine, Vanderlyn R. *The American funeral theater: an analysis of the organization of funeral directing*. New York: Appleton-Century-Crofts, 1971.

Pine, Vanderlyn R. *Caretaker of the dead*. New York: Halsted Pr., 1975.

Polner, Murray and Arthur Barron. *The questions children ask*. New York: MacMillan, 1964.

Polson, Cyril J. *The disposal of the dead*. 2d rev. ed. Springfield, Illinois: C.C. Thomas Co., 1962.

Polson, Cyril J. *Essentials of forensic medicine*. 2d ed. rev. and illus. Elmsford, New York: Pergamon Press, 1965.

Pool, David de Sola. *Why I am a Jew*. New York: Bloch, 1951.

Poteet, G. Howard. *Death and dying, a bibliography, 1950-1974*. Troy, New York: Witson Publishing Co., 1976.

Prentice, A.E. *Suicide; a selective bibliography*. Metuchen, New Jersey: Scarecrow, 1974.

Pretzel, Paul W. *Understanding the suicidal person*. Nashville: Abingdon Pr., 1972.

Price, Julius J. *Rabbinic conceptions about death*. Chicago: Open Court Pr., 1920.

Puckle, Bertram S. *Funeral customs, their origin and development*. Detroit: Singing Tree Press, 1968.

Pugsley, Clement H. *In sorrow's lone hour*. Nashville, Tennessee: Abingdon, 1963.

Quint, Jeanne C. *The nurse and the dying patient*. New York: MacMilan, 1967.

Rabin, Gil. *Changes*. New York: Harper & Row Publishers, 1973.

Rabinowicz. H. *A guide to life, Jewish laws and customs of mourning*. London: Jewish Chronicle Publications, 1964.

Raether, Howard C. and Robert C. Slater. *The funeral director and his role as a counselor*. Milwaukee, Wisconsin: National Funeral Directors Association, 1975.

Raether, Howard C. *Successful funeral service practice*. Englewood Cliffs, New Jersey: Prentice-Hall Publishing Co., 1971.

Rahner, Karl. *On the theology of death*. New York: Seabury Pr., Inc., 1961.

Ramos, Suzanne. *Teaching your child to cope with crisis*. New York: David McKay Co., Inc., 1974.

Ramsey, Paul. *The patient as person: explorations in medical ethics*. New Haven: Yale University Pr., 1970.

Rawlings, Marjorie Kinnan. *The yearling*. New York: Scribner's, 1939. Children's book.

Reed, Elizabeth L. *Helping children with the mystery of death*. Nashville, Tennessee: Abingdon Press, 1970.

Reeves, Robert P. et. al. *Pastoral care of the dying and bereaved; selected readings*. New York: Health Sciences Pub. Corp., 1973.

Reik, Theodor. *Curiosities of the self*. New York: Farrar, Strauss & Giraux, 1965.

Rezek, Philipp R. *Autopsy pathology, a guide for pathologists and clinicians*. Springfield, Illinois: C.C. Thomas Co., 1963.

Reingold, Joseph C. *Fear of being a woman*. New York: Grune & Stratton, 1964.

Reinhardt, James M. *The psychology of strange killers*. Springfield, Illinois: Charles C. Thomas, 1962.

Resnik, H.L.P. ed. *The diagnosis and management of the suicidal individual*. Boston: Little, Brown, 1967.

Rheingold, Joseph C. *The mother, anxiety, and death; the catastrophic death complex*. 1st ed. Boston: Little, Brown and Co., 1967.

Riemer, Jack ed. *Jewish reflections on death*. New York: Schocken Books, Inc., 1974.

Riese, W. *The conception of disease*. New York: Philosophical Library, Inc., 1953.

Rilke, Rainer M. *The notebooks of Malte Laurids Brigge*. New York: W.W. Norton, 1964.

Rinald, C.L. *Dark dreams*. New York: Harper and Row, 1974.

Rite of funerals. Washington, D.C.: United States Catholic Conference, 1971.

Robertson, Alec. *Requiem; music of mourning and consolation*. New York: Praeger, 1968.

Robinson, Haddon W. *Grief.* Grand Rapids, Michigan: Zondervan Publishing House, 1976.

Rochlin, Gregory. *Griefs and discontents: the forces of change.* Boston: Little, Brown & Co., 1965.

Rogers, William F. *Ye shall be comforted.* Philadelphia: Westminster Press, 1950.

Rogness, Alvin N. *Appointment with death.* Nashville, Tennessee: Thomas Nelson, Inc., 1972.

Rosenbaum, Ernest H. *Living with cancer.* New York: Praeger Pubs., Inc., 1975.

Rosenblum, J. *A child psychologist talks to parents on a difficult subject.* International Order of the Golden Rule, 1963.

Rosenblum, J. *How to explain death to a child.* International Order of the Golden Rule, 1963.

Rosenfeld, Albert. *Prolongevity.* Westminster, Maryland: Alfred A. Knopf, Inc., 1976.

Rosenfeld, A. *The second genesis: the coming control of life.* New Jersey: Prentice-Hall, Inc., 1969.

Ross, Joan *Post-mortem appearances.* 6th ed. New York: Oxford University Press, 1963.

Ross, W.D. *The right and the good.* Clarendon: Oxford University Pr., 1930.

Rotering, Robert ed. *To love forever. Thoughts on death and life.* Winona, Minnesota: St. Mary's College Press, 1971.

Roth, J. *Timetables.* Indianapolis: The Bobbs-Merrill Co., Inc., 1963.

Royce, Josiah. *The conception of immortality.* New York: Greenwood Press, 1968.

Ruitenbeek, Hendrik M. ed. *Death: interpretations.* New York: Delta Books, 1969.

Rush, Alfred Clement. *Death and burial in Christian antiquity.* Washington, D.C.: The Catholic University of America Pr., 1941.

Russell, O. Ruth. *Freedom to die.* New York: Human Sciences Pr., 1975.

St. John-Stevas, N. *Life, death and the law.* New York: Meridian Books, 1961.

Salten, F. *Bambi.* New York: Grosset & Dunlap, 1969. Children's book.

Sanyal, J.M. trans. *The Srimad-Bhagavatam*. London: Luzac & Co., 1929-1939.
Saunders, Cicely. *Care of the dying*. London: MacMillan & Co., Ltd, 1959.
Scherzer, Carl J. *Ministering to the dying*. Englewood Cliffs, N.J.: Prentice-Hall, Inc., 1963.
Schmeck, H.M., Jr. *The semi-artificial man: a dawning revolution in medicine*. New York: Walker & Co., 1965.
Schoenberg, Bernard ed. *Anticipatory grief*. New York: Columbia University Press, 1974.
Schoenberg, Bernard et. al. ed. *Bereavement: its psychosocial aspects*. New York: Columbia University Pr., 1975.
Schoenberg, Bernard et. al. *Loss and grief: psychological management in medical practice*. New York: Columbia University Pr., 1970.
Schoenberg, Bernard et. al. *Psychosocial aspects of terminal care*. New York: Columbia University Pr., 1972.
Schur, Max. *Freud; living and dying*. New York: International Universities Pr., 1972.
Scientific America. *Life and death and medicine*. San Francisco: W.H. Freeman and Co., 1973.
Scott, Frances and Ruth Brewer. *Confrontations of death; a book of readings and a suggested method of instruction*. Corvallis: Continuing Education Publications, Oregon State University, 1971.
Scott, Nathan A. comp. *The modern vision of death*. Richmond, Virginia: John Knox, 1967.
Seagren, Daniel. *Letters to Chip*. Grand Rapids, Michigan: Zondervan Publishing House, 1969.
Segal, Erich. *Love story*. New York: Harper and Row, Publishers, 1970.
Seligman, Martin E.P. *Helplessness*. San Francisco: W.H. Freeman & Co., 1975.
Seskin, Jane. *Young widow*. New York: Ace Books, 1975.
Sexton, Anne. *The awful rowing toward God*. Boston, Massachusetts: Houghton Mifflin, 1975.
Shaler, Nathaniel Southgate. *The individual: a study of life and death*. New York: D. Appleton & Co., 1901.
Shastri, J.L. ed. *The Siva Purana*. Delhi: Motilal Banarsidass, 1970.

Shepard, Martin. *Someone you love is dying.* New York: Harmony Books, 1975.
Sherrill, Helen H. and Lewis J. Sherrill. *Interpreting death to children.* Riverside, New York: National Council of the Churches Christ, 1956.
Shetrone, H.C. *The mound builders.* New York: D. Appleton & Co., 1930.
Shibles, Warren. *Death: an interdisciplinary analysis.* Whitewater, Wisconsin: Language Pr., 1974.
Shneidman, E.S. ed. *Essays in self-destruction.* New York: International Science Pr., 1967.
Shneidman, E.S. and N.L. Farberow ed. *Clues to suicide.* New York: McGraw-Hill, 1957.
Shneidman, Edwin S. ed. *Death and the college student.* New York: Behavioral Publications, 1972.
Shneidman, Edwin S. *Death: current perspectives.* Palo Alto, California: Mayfield Publishing Co., 1976.
Shneidman, Edwin S. *Deaths of man.* New York: Quadrangle/ The New York Times Book Co., 1973.
Shultz, Gladys. *Widows wise and otherwise.* New York: Lippincott, 1949.
Silverberg, Robert. *Mound builders of ancient America; the archaeology of a myth.* Greenwich, Connecticut: New York Graphic Society, 1968.
Silverman, Phyllis R. *Helping each other in widowhood.* New York: Health Sciences Pub. Corp., 1974.
Silverman, Phyllis R. *If you will lift the load; a guide to the creation of widowed to widowed programs.* New York: Health Sciences Pub. Corp., 1966.
Simmons, L. *The role of the aged in primitive societies.* New Haven: Yale Universities Pr., 1945.
Simpson, Cedric K. *Forensic medicine.* 6th ed. London: E. Arnold, c1969.
Simpson, Cedric K. *Modern trends in forensic medicine.* New York: Appleton, 1967.
Simpson, M. *Theology of death and eternal life.* Cork: Mercier Pr., 1971.
Slote, Alfred. *Hang tough, Paul Mather.* New York: J.B. Lippincott Co., 1973. Children's book.

Smith, Doris Buchanan. *A taste of blackberries*. New York: Thomas Y. Crowell Co., 1973. Children's book.

Smith, H.L. *Ethics and the new medicine*. New York: Abingdon Pr., 1970.

Smith, Ivan. *The death of a wombat*. New York: Charles Scribner's Sons, 1972. Children's book.

Smith, Joanne Kelley. *Free fall*. Valley Forge: Judson Press, 1975.

Snively, William D. *Sea within; the story of our body fluid*. Philadelphia: Lippincott, 1960.

Snow, Louis Wheeler. *A death with dignity, when the Chinese came*. New York: Random House, 1974.

Snyder, Lemoyne et. al. *Homicide investigation*. Springfield, Illinois: C.C. Thomas, 1944.

Soulen, Richard N. ed. *Care for the dying*. Atlanta, Georgia: John Knox Pr., 1974.

Spiro, Jack D. *A time to mourn*. New York: Bloch, 1967.

Spitz, Rene. *The first year of life*. New York: International Universities Pr., 1965.

Spriggs, A.O. *The art and science of embalming*. Springfield, Ohio: Champion Co., 1963.

Spriggs, A.O. *Champion restorative art*. Springfield, Ohio: Champion Co., 1968.

Sprott, S.E. *The English debate on suicide from Donne to Hume*. La Salle, Illinois: Open Court Publishing Co., 1961.

Standard S. and H. Nathan. *Should the patient know the truth?* New York: Springer Publishing Co., Inc., 1955.

Stanek, Murial. *I won't go without a father*. Chicago: Whitman, 1972. Children's book.

Starenko, Ronald C. *God, grass and grace*. St. Louis, Missouri: Concordia Publishing House, 1975.

Start, Clarissa. *When you're a widow*. St. Louis: Concordia, 1968.

Statistical abstract of funeral service facts and figures of the United States. 1972 ed. Milwaukee, Wisconsin: National Funeral Directors Association, 1972.

Stein, Sara Bonnett. *About dying*. New York: Walker & Co., 1974.

Steinberg, Milton. *Basic Judaism*. New York: Harcourt, 1947.

Steinfels, Peter and Robert W. Veatch. *Death inside out; the Hastings Center report*. New York: Harper and Row Publishers, 1975.

Stendahl, Dristen ed. *Immortality and resurrection*. New York: MacMillan Co., 1965.

Stengel, Erwin. *Suicide and attempted suicide*. Baltimore: Penguin Books, 1964.

Stephens, Simon. *Death comes home*. New York: Morehouse-Barlow Co., Inc., 1973.

Stinnette, Charles R. *Anxiety and faith*. Greenwich, Connecticut: Seabury Pr., Inc., 1955.

Stolz, Mary. *By the highway home*. New York: Harper and Row Publishers, 1971.

Stone, Howard W. *Suicide and grief*. Philadelphia: Fortress Press, 1972.

Strauss, Anselm and Barney Glaser. *Anguish, a case history of a dying trajectory*. Mill Valley, California: The Sociology Pr., 1970.

Strub, Clarence G. *The principles and practice of embalming*. 4th ed. Dallas: L.G. Frederick, 1967.

Strugnell, Cecile. *Adjustment to widowhood, and some related problems; a selected, annotated bibliography*. New York: Health Sciences Pub. Corp., 1974.

Studies of Kennedy's assassination. Washington, D.C.: Bureau of Social Science Research, 1966.

Stull, E.C. *My turtle died today*. New York: Holt, Rinehart and Winston, 1964. Children's book.

Sudnow, David. *Passing on: the social organization of dying*. Englewood Cliffs, New Jersey: Prentice-Hall, Inc., 1967.

Sulzberger, Cyrus L. *My brother death*. New York: Harper, 1961.

Switzer, David K. *The dynamics of grief: its source, pain and healing*. Nashville, Tennessee: Abingdon Press, 1970.

Taves, Isabella. *Love must not be wasted*. New York: Thomas Y. Crowell Co., 1974.

Taves, Isabella. *Women alone*. New York: Funk and Wagnalls, 1968.

Theilicke, Helmut. *Death and life*. Philadelphia: Fortress Press, 1970.

Thompson, Edward John. *Suttee: a historical and philosophical enquiry into the Hindu rite of widow burning*. London: G. Allen and Unwin, 1928.

Tillich, P. *The courage to be*. New Haven: Yale University Pr., 1952.

Torrie, Margaret. *Begin again: a book for women alone*. London: J.M. Dent, 1970.

Tournier, Paul. *The meaning of grief*. Richmond, Virginia: John Knox, 1968.

Toynbee, Arnold ed. *Man's concern with death*. New York: McGraw-Hill Book Co., 1968.

Tresselt, Alvin. *The dead tree*. New York: Parent's Magazine Press, 1972. Children's book.

Trubo, Richard. *An act of mercy: euthanasia today*. Los Angeles: Nash Publishing, 1973.

Turnage, Mac. N. and Ann Shaw Turnage. *More than you dare to ask; the first year of living with cancer*. Atlanta, Georgia: John Knox Pr., 1976.

Turner, Ann Warren. *Houses for the dead*. New York: David McKay Co., Inc., 1976.

Ujhely, Gertrud B. *The nurse and her problem patients*. New York: Springer, 1963.

Ulanov, Barry. *Death - a book of preparation and consolation*. New York: Sheed and Ward, 1959.

Van Gennep, Arnold. *The rites of passage*. London: Routledge and Kegan Paul, 1960.

Vaughan, John S. *Life after death*. New York: Benzinger Brothers, Inc., 1902.

Veatch, Robert M. *Death, dying and the biological revolution. Our last quest for responsibility*. New Haven: Yale University Pr., 1976.

Vernon, Glenn M. *Sociology of death; an analysis of death-related behavior*. New York: Ronald Pr., 1970.

Verwoerdt, Adriaan. *Communication with the fatally ill*. Springfield, Illinois: Charles C. Thomas, Publisher, 1966.

Viorst, Judith. *The tenth good thing about Barney*. Montreal: McClelland and Stewart Publishers, 1971. Children's book.

Vogel, Linda J. *Helping A Child Understand Death*. Philadelphia: Fortress Press, 1975.

Vulliamy, Colwyn Edward. *Immortal man - a study of funeral customs and of beliefs in regard to the nature and fate of the soul*. London: Metheun and Co., 1926.

Wagner, Johannes ed. *Reforming the rites of death*. New York: Paulist-Newman, 1968.

Wagner, Richard E. *Death and taxes*. California: American Enterprise Pr., 1973.

Wahl, Charles W. ed. *Management of death and the dying patient book: dimensions in psychosomatic medicine.* Boston: Little, Brown & Co., 1964.

Wahl, Charles W., R. Leslie and N. Kennedy. *Helping the dying patient and his family.* New York: National Association of Social Workers, 1960.

Walker, Kenneth M. *The circle of life: a search for an attitude to pain, disease, old age and death.* College Park, Maryland: McGrath Publishing Co., 1970.

Warburg, Sandol S. *Growing time.* Boston: Houghton Mifflin Co., 1969. Children's book.

Warner, W.L. *The living and the dead.* New Haven: Yale University Pr., 1959.

Watson, Lyall. *The romeo error, a matter of life and death.* Garden City, New York: Doubleday Publishing Co., 1975.

Watts, Alan. *Death.* Millbrae, California: Celestial Arts, 1975.

Watts, Richard C. *Straight talk about death with young people.* Philadelphia, Pennsylvania: Westminster Pr., 1975.

Waugh, E. *The loved one: an American tragedy.* London: Chapman & Hall, 1948.

Weatherhead, Leslie D. *Wounded spirits.* New York: Abingdon Press, 1963.

Wecht, Cyril H. *Legal medicine annual.* New York: Appleton-Century-Crofts, 1969-1972.

Weisman, A.D. and R. Kastenbaum. *The psychological autopsy: a study of the terminal phases of life.* New York: Behavioral Publications, 1968.

Weisman, Avery D. *The existential core of psychoanalysis.* Boston: Little, Brown, Inc., 1965.

Weisman, Avery D. *On dying and denying.* New York: Behavioral Publications, 1972.

Weisman, Avery D. *The realization of death; a guide for the psychological autopsy.* New York: Jason Aronson, Inc., 1974.

Weiss, Jess. *The vestibule.* Port Washington, N.Y.: Ashley Books, Inc., 1972.

Wentz, Walter Yeeling Evans. *Das Tibetanische totenbuch.* Zurich: Rascher Verlag, 1953.

Werkman, Sidney L. *Only a little time: a memoir of my wife.* Boston: Little, Brown and Co., 1972.

Wernecke, Herbert H. *When loved ones are called home*. Grand Rapids, Michigan: Baker Book House, 1951.
Wertenbaker, L. Tucker. *Death of a man*. Boston: Beacon Press, 1957.
Westberg, Granger. *Good grief*. Philadelphia: Fortress Press, 1971.
Westburg, Granger. *Minister and doctor meet*. New York: Harpers, 1961.
White, E.B. *Charlotte's Web*. New York: Harper and Row, 1952. Children's book.
Whitehead, Ruth. *The mother tree*. New York: The Seabury Press, 1971. Children's book.
Wieman, Henry N. *The source of human good*. Carbondale, Illinois: Southern Illinois University Pr., 1946.
Williams, Glanville L. *The sanctity of life and the criminal*. New York: Knopf, 1957.
Williams, Melvin G. *The last word: lure and lore of early New England Cemeteries*. Boston, Massachusetts: Oldstone Enterprises, 1973.
Williams, Phillip W. *When a loved one dies*. Minneapolis, Minnesota: Augusburg Publishing House, 1976.
Williams, Robert H. ed. *To live and to die: when, why, and how*. New York: Springer-Verlag, 1974.
Wilson, Jerry B. *Death by decision*. Philadelphia, Pennsylvania: Westminster Pr., 1975.
Windsor, Patricia. *The summer before*. New York: Harper and Row, 1973. Children's book.
Winter, Arthur ed. *The moment of death, a symposium*. Springfield, Illinois: C.C. Thomas Co., 1969.
Winter, David. *Hereafter, what happens after death.* Wheaton, Illinois: Harold Shaw Publishers and the Christian Promotion Trust, 1972.
Wolf, Anna M. *Helping your child to understand death*. New York: Child Study Pr., 1973.
Wolfenstein, Martha and Gilbert Kliman ed. *Children and the death of a president*. Garden City, New York: Doubleday & Co., Inc., 1965.
Wolitzer, Hilma. *Ending*. New York: MacMillan Inc., 1975.
Wolstenholme, G.E.W. and M. O'Connor ed. *Ethics in medical progress with special reference to transplantation.* **Boston:** Little, Brown & Co., 1966.

Wood, Charles R. comp. *Sermon outlines for funeral services*. Grand Rapids, Michigan: Kregel Publications, 1970.

Woodson, Meg. *If I die at 30*. Grand Rapids, Michigan: Zondervan Publishing House, 1975.

Worcester, Alfred. *The care of the aged, the dying and the dead*. 2d ed. Springfield, Illinois: C.C. Thomas Co., c 1961.

Wright, H.T. *The Matthew tree*. New York: Pantheon Books, Inc., 1975.

Wyschogroc, Edith. *The Phenomenon of death, faces of mortality*. New York: Harper Colophon Books, Harper and Row Publishers, 1973.

Young, Jim. *When the whale came to my town*. New York: Alfred A. Knopf, 1974. Children's book.

Zeligs, Rose. *Children's experience with death*. Springfield, Illinois: Charles C. Thomas, Publisher, 1974.

Zim, Herbert S. and Sonia Bleeker. *Life and death*. New York: William Morrow and Co., 1970.

Zlotnik, Dov ed., tr. *Tractote mourning (semahot); regulations relating to death, burial and mourning*. New Haven, Connecticut: Yale University Press, 1966.

Zolotow, Charlotte. *My grandson Lew*. New York: Harper, 1974. Children's book.

MISCELLANEOUS

Transparency "Death", Creative Visuals, Box 1991, Big Spring, TX 78729, $6/copy

Audio Tape Reel "Personality Theory and Death", 30 minutes, McGraw Hill Book Co., 1221 Avenue of the Americas, New York, NY 10020, $10/copy.

Videotape "Roundabout: Living or Dead", 15 minutes, National TV Center, Box A, Blood ington, IN 47401, S35/copy.

Audio Cassette "Death of a Salesman", 44 minutes, Center of Cassette Studios, 8110 Webb Avenue, North Hollywood, CA 91605, $18.95/copy.

Audio Tape Reed "Civil Disorders and the Impact of the Death Penalty", 15 minutes, Pacifica tape, Department PS 74, 5316 Venice Blvd., Los Angeles, CA 90019.

"Perspectives on Death: A Thematic Teaching Unit", Contains an audio-visual package, an anthology of readings, a student activity book and a teacher's resource booklet. The Library Filmstrip Center, 3033 Aloma, Wichita, KS 67211.

"Instructional Resources for Teaching the Psychology of Death and Dying" by S. Shapiro, Order No. MS No. 460, A compilation of instructional resources including: discussion topics, class exercises and projects, community projects, questionnaires, a syllabus, etc., Journal Supplement Abstract Service, American Psychological Association, 1200 Seventeenth Street, N.W., Washington, D.C. 20036, $3/copy.

"Death", An Audio-visual packet with five filmstrips, a record or cassettes, audio-visual packet with five filmstrips, a record or cassettes, audio script booklets and a discussion guide. Parent's Magazine Films, Inc., 52 Vanderbilt Avenue, New York, NY 10017, $49/copy with record, $58/copy with cassettes.

CHAPTERS AND ARTICLES IN BOOKS

"Aging", In *Developmental psychology today*. Del Mar, California: Communications Research Machines, Inc., 1971. 497-511.

Alexander, I.E. and A.M. Adlerstein. "Studies in the psychology of death". In Henry P. David and J.C. Brengelmann ed. *Perspectives in personality research*. New York: Springer Publishing Co., 1960. 65-92.

Alpert, Augusta. "A brief communication on children's reactions to the assassination of the President". In v. 19 of *The psychoanalytic study of the child*. New York: International Universities Press, 1964.

Anthony, E. James ed. "The child in his family". In v. 2 of *The impact of disease and death*. New York: Wiley and Sons, 1973.

Bacon, Francis. "Of death". in v. 2 of S.H. Reynolds ed. *Bacon's essays*. Oxford: Clarendon Pr., 1890. 12-18.

Barnes, Marion J. "Reactions to the death of a mother".In v. 19 of *The Psychoanalytic Study of the Child.* New York: International Universities Press, Inc., 1964.

Bender, Lauretta. *Aggression, hostility and anxiety in children.* Springfield, Illinois: C.C. Thomas, 1953. 40-65.

Benoliel, Jeanne Quint. "Talking to patients about death". Chapter 36 in Barbara W. Spradley. *Contemporary community nursing.* Boston: Little, Brown and Co., 1975. 306-314.

Berando, Felix M. "Widowhood status in the United States: perspective on a neglected aspect of the family life cycle". In Jacqueline P. Wiseman ed. *People and partners.* San Francisco: Canfield Press, 1971, 458-466.

Beres, David and Samuel J. Obers. "The effects of extreme deprivation in infancy on psychic structures in adolescence". In v. 5 of *The psychoanalytic study of the child.* New York: International Universities Pr., 1950. 212-235.

Brantl, George ed. *Great religions of modern man: Catholicism.* New York: A Washington Square Press Book, 1961. pp. 246-267.

Camus, Albert. *The stranger.* New York: Vintage Books, 1958. 24.

Carrel, Alexis. "The mystery of death". In I. Galdston ed. *Medicine and mankind.* New York: Appleton-Century, 1936.

"The child with a fatal illness". Chapter 17 in Peggy L. Chinn. *Child health maintenance.* St. Louis, Missouri: C.V. Mosby Co., 1974. 430-444.

Ch'ung, Wang. "On death". In his *Lun heng* (critical essays) translated by Alfred Forke. New York: Paragon Book Gallery, 1962.

"Dead", "Death", and "Death rates". In v. 7 of *The Encyclopedia Britannica.* Chicago: William Benton, 1961. 96-98; 108-114.

"Death in a child in the emergency department". In Robert M. Reece and John W. Chamberlain. *Manual of emergency pediatrics.* Philadelphia: W.B. Saunders Co., 1974. 87.

"Death". In v. 8 of *The Encyclopedia Americana.* New York: American Corporation, 1959. 539-444.

"Death, the last developmental stage". Chapter 10 in Ruth Murray and Judith Zentner. *Nursing assessment and health promotion through the life span.* Englewood Cliffs, New Jersey: Prentice-Hall, Inc., 1975. 323-344.

Deutsch, Helene. "A two-year-old boy's first love comes to grief". In L. Jessner and E. Pavenstedt ed. *Dynamics of Psychopathology in Childhood.* New York: Grune and Stratton, 1959.

Durkheim, E. *Elementary forms of religious life.* New York: Free Pr., 1947. 397.

"The dying child, his parents and the nurse". Chapter 24 in A. Joy Ingalls and M. Constance Salerno. *Maternal and child health nursing*. 3d ed. St. Louis, Missouri: C.V. Mosby Co., 1975. 359.

Dobzhansky, Theodosius. "Religion, death and evolutionary adaptation" in Melford E. Spiro ed. *The context and meaning of cultural anthropology*. New York: The Free Press, 1965. 61-73.

Eliot, Thomas D. "Adjusting to the death of a loved one". In Barbara Chesser and Ava A. Gray. *Marriage, creating a partnership*. Dubuque, Iowa: Kendall/Hunt Publishing Co., 1975. 184-188.

Eliot, Thomas D. "Bereavement: inevitable but not unsurmountable". In H. Becker and R. Hill ed. *Family, marriage and parenthood*. Boston: Heath, 1955. 641-668.

Fairbairn, Ronald D. "The war neuroses - their nature and significance (1943)". In *Object relations theory of the personality*. New York: Basic Books, 1954. 256-288.

Farberow, Norman L., Samuel M. Heilig and Robert E. Titman. "Training manual for telephone evaluation and emergency management of suicidal persons". In *Technique in crisis intervention: a training manual*. Los Angeles: Suicide Prevention Center, Inc., December, 1968. 2-16.

Farberow, Norman and Robert E. Litman. "Suicide prevention". In H.L.P. Resnick and H.L. Ruben ed. *Emergency psychiatric care: the management of mental health crises*. New York: Charles Pr., 1974. 105-118.

Feifel, Herman. "Death". In v. 2 of A. Deutsch ed. *The encyclopedia of mental health*. New York: Franklin Watts, 1963. 427-450.

Feifel, Herman. "Death - relevant variable in psychology" in Rollo May ed. *Existential psychology*. New York: Random House, Inc., 1961.

Fenichel, Otto. "A critique of the death instinct". In v. 1 of *The collected papers of Otto Fenichel*. New York: W.W. Norton and Co., 1953. 363-372.

Fletcher, J.F. "Euthanasia, our right to die". In *Morals and Medicine*. New Jersey: Princeton University Pr., 1954.

Forde, D. "Death and succession: an analysis of Yako mortuary ritual". In Max Gluckman ed. *Essays on the ritual of social relations*. Manchester: Manchester University Pr., 1962. 89-123.

Fox, R.C. "A sociological perspective on organ transplantation and hemodialysis". In I. Ladimer ed. *New dimensions in legal and ethical concepts for human research. Annals of the New York Academy of Science*, 169: 406-428, 1970.

Freud, Anna. "Discussion of 'grief and mourning in infancy and early childhood' by Bowlby". In Ruth S. Eissler et. al. ed. *The psychoanalytic study of the child*. New York: International Universities Pr., Inc., 1960. 53-94.

Freud, Anna. "The shock of separation". In *War and Children*. New York: International Universities Pr., 1944.

Freud, Anna, in collaboration with Sophie Dann. "An experiment in group upbringing". In v. 6 of Ruth S. Eissler et. al. ed. *Psychoanalytic study of the child*. New York: International Universities Pr., Inc., 1951. 127-169.

Freud, Sigmund. "Beyond the pleasure principle". In v. 18 of *Collected papers* Standard edition. London: Hogarth, 1955. 7-64.

Freud, Sigmund. "Dreams of the death of persons of whom the dreamer is fond". In v. 4 of *Collected papers*. Standard edition. London: Hogarth, 1953.

Freud, Sigmund. "Inhibitions, symptoms and anxiety". In v. 20 of *Collected papers*. Standard edition. London: Hogarth, 1959. 87-174.

Freud, Sigmund. "Doestoevsky and parricide". In v. 5 of *Collected papers*. New York: Basic Books, 1959. 222-242.

Freud, Sigmund, "Our attitude towards death". In *Collected papers*. London: Hogarth, 1956. 304-317.

Freud, Sigmund. "The theme of the three caskets". In v. 4 of *Collected papers*. New York: Basic Books, 1959. 152-170.

Freud, S. "Thoughts for the times on war and death". In v. 4 of *Collected Papers*. London: Hogarth Pr., 1948.

Freud, Sigmund. "The uncanny". In v. 4 of *Collected papers*. New York: Basic Books, 1959. 368-407.

Fried, M. "Grieving for a lost home". In J.L. Duhl ed. *The environment of the metropolis*. New York: Basic Books, 1962.

Fulton, Robert. "Contemporary funeral practices". In Howard C. Raether ed. *Modern funeral practice*. New York: Prentice-Hall, 1971. 289-320.

Fulton, R. and J. Fulton. "A psycho-social aspect of terminal care: anticipatory grief". In Bernard Schoenberg et. al. ed. *Psychological aspects of terminal care*. New York: Columbia Pr., 1972. 227-242.

Furman, Erna. "Treatment of under-fives by way of their parents". In v. 12 of *The psychoanalytic study of the child*. New York: International Universities Pr., Inc., 1957.

Furman, Robert A. "Death and the young child". In v. 19 of *The psychoanalytic study of the child*. New York: International Universities Pr., Inc., 1964.

Furman, Robert A. "Death of a six-year-old's mother during his analysis". In v. 19 of *The psychoanalytic study of the child*, New York: International Universities Pr., Inc., 1964.

Giovannitti, L. *The prisoners of Combine D*. New York: Bantam Books, Inc., 1959. 278-279.

Gluckman, Max. "Rituals of rebellion in South-east Africa". In *Rituals of rebellion*. Manchester: Manchester University Pr., 1954. 1-36.

Goffman, E. *Behavior in public places*. New York: Free Pr., 1963. 126.

Goffman, E. *Encounters*. Indianapolis: The Bobbs-Merrill Co., Inc., 1961. 55-61.

Goffman, E. *Presentation of self in everyday life*. Garden City, New York: Doubleday & Co., Inc., 1959. 151-152.

Goodman, Paul. "On the intellectual inhibition of explosive grief and anger". In *Utopian essays and practical proposals*, New York: Random House, 1962.

Gorer, G. "The pornography of death". In Maurice Stein, Arthur Vidich and David White ed. *Identity and anxiety: survival of the person in mass society*. New York: The Free Pr., 1960. 402-407.

Gorer, Geoffrey. "The pornography of death". In W. Phillips and P. Rahv ed. *Modern writing*. New York: McGraw-Hill, 1959. 157-188.

Green, and A. J. Solnit. "The pediatric management of the dying child. Pt. 2, The child's reaction to the fear of dying". In *Modern perspectives in child development*. New York: International Universities Pr., Inc., 1963. 217-228.

Grotjahn, Martin. "About the representation of death in the art of antiquity and in the unconscious of modern man". In George B.

Wilbur and Warner Muensterberger ed. *Psychoanalysis and culture*. New York: International University Pr., 1951. 410-424.

Gyomroi, Edith Ludowyk. "The analysis of a young concentration camp victim". In v. 18 of Ruth S. Issler et. al. ed. *The psychoanalytic study of the child*. New York: International Universities Pr., Inc., 1963. 484-510.

Hamburger, J. and J. Crosnier. "Moral and ethical problems in transplantation". In F.T. Rapport and J. Dausset ed. *Human transplantation*. New York: Grune & Stratton, Inc., 1968. 37-44.

Hartland, E. Sidney. "Death and the disposal of the dead". In v. 4 of James Hastings ed. *Encyclopedia of religion and ethics*. New York: C. Scribner's Sons, 1912. 411-444.

Heilig, S.M. and David J. Klugman. "The social worker in a suicide prevention center". In Howard J. Parad ed. *Crisis intervention: selected readings*. New York: Family Service Association of America, 1965. 274-283.

Hellman, Ilse. "Hampstead nursery follow-up studies - 1. Sudden separation and its effect followed over twenty years". In v. 17 of Ruth S. Essler et. al. ed. *The psychoanalytic study of the child*. New York: International Pr., Inc., 1962. 159-174.

Hertz, Robert. "A contribution to the study of the collective representation of death". In *Death and the right hand* (translated from the French by Rodney and Claudia Needham). Glencoe, Illinois: Free Pr., 1960. 29-86.

Hocart, A.M. "Death customs". In v. 5 of *The Encyclopedia of the Social Sciences*. New York: MacMillan Co., 1931. 21-27.

Hunt, Leigh. "Death of little children (and) on the realities of imagination". In v. 27 of *The Harvard classics*. New York: P. F. Collier & Son, 1910. 299-310.

Hurlock, Elizabeth B. "Concepts of death". In *Child development*. 5th ed. New York: McGraw-Hill Book Co., 1972. 354-355.

Jacobson, David S. "Death". In v. 3 of *The universal Jewis encyclopedia*. New York: Universal Jewish Encyclopedia Co., 1943.

Jones, Ernest. "Dying together". In v. 1 of *Essays in applied psychoanalysis*. London: Hogarth Pr., 1951.

Kastenbaum, Robert. "Engrossment and perspective in later life: a developmenta-field approach" in Robert Kastenbaum ed. *Contributions to the psychobiology of aging*. New York: McGraw-Hill, Inc., 1959. 1-18.

Kastenbaum, Robert and Avery D. Weisman, "The psychological autopsy as a reasearch procedure in gerontology". In Donald P. Kent, Robert Kastenbaum and Sylvia Sherwood ed. *Research planning and action for the elderly*. New York: Behavioral Publications, Inc., 1972. 210-217.

Kastenbaum, Robert J. "Loving, dying and other gerontologic addenda". In Eisdorfer, Carl and M. Powell Lawton. *The psychology of adult development and aging*. Washington, D.C.: American Psychological Association, 1973. 699-708.

Keeler, W.R. "Children's reaction to the death of a parent". In P.H. Hoch and J. Zubin ed. *Depression*. New York: Grune and Stratton, 1954. 109-120.

Keyfitz, Nathan. "Changes of birth and death rates and their demographic effects". In *Rapid population growth: consequences and policy implications*. Baltimore: Johns Hopkins University Pr., 1971. 639-680.

Klein, Melanie. "Mourning and its relation to manic-depressive states". *Contributions to psychoanalysis*. London: Hogarth, 1948. 311-338.

Klemer, Richard H. and Rebecca M. Smith. "Death". Chapter in *Marriage and family relationships*. New York: Harper and Row, 1970.

Kubler-Ross, Elisabeth. "Crisis management of dying persons and their families". Chapter 8 in H.L.P. Resnick and H.L. Ruben. *Emergency psychiatric care: the management of mental health crises*. New York: Charles Pr., 1974. 143-156.

Kubler-Ross, Elisabeth. "Death". In v. 5 of *The Encyclopedia Britannica*, 1974. 526-529.

Kubler-Ross, Elisabeth. "Dying as a human psychological event". In Greinacher, Norton and Alois Mueller. *The experience of dying*. New York: Herder and Herder, 1974.

Kubler-Ross, Elisabeth. "Facing death". Chapter 25 in John G. Howells ed. *Modern perspectives in the psychiatry of old age*. New York: Brunner and Mazel, 1975. 531-539.

Kubler-Ross, Elisabeth. "Facing up to death". In *Annual editions: readings in human development*, 1973-74 edition. Guilford, Connecticut: Dushkin Publishing Group, Inc., 1975-76. 237-239.

Kubler-Ross, Elisabeth. "The five stages of dying". In *Encyclopedia Science Supplement*. New York: Grolier, Inc., 1971. 92-97.

Kubler-Ross, Elisabeth. "Lessons from the dying". In *Sociologico de la muerte*. Madrid, Spain, 1974. 15-24. (First published in *Tribuna Medica*, Madrid, Spain, 1973).

Kubler-Ross, Elisabeth. "Psychotherapy for the dying patient". In v. 5 of J.H. Masserman ed. *Current psychiatric therapies*. New York: Grune & Stratton, Inc., 1970. 110-117.

Kuhn, R. "The attempted murder of a prostitute". In Rollo May ed. *Existence*. New York: Basic Books, 1958.

Kurt, Wolff. *The biological, sociological and psychological aspects of aging*. Springfield, Illinois: Charles C. Thomas, 1959. 7.

Lessa, William A. "Death customs and rites". In v. 7 of *Collier's Encyclopedia*. New York: MacMillan Educational Corp., 757-765.

Leviton, Daniel. "Death, bereavement and suicide education". In Donald Read ed. *New directions in health education*. New York: MacMillan, 1971. 170-203.

Lindemann, Erich. "Modifications in the course of ulcerative colitis in relationship to changes in life situations and reaction patterns". In H.G. Wolff ed. *Life stress and bodily disease*. Baltimore: Williams and Wilkins Co., 1950. 706-723.

Lindeman, Erich. "Psychosocial factors as stressor agent". In J.M. Tanner ed. *Stress and psychiatric discrder*. Oxford: Blackwell Scientific Publications, 1960.

Lopata, Helena Znaniecki. "Role changes in widowhood: a world perspective". In Donald O. Cowgill and Lowell D. Holmes ed. *Aging and modernization*. New York: Meredith Corporation, 1972.

"Loss, grief and death". Chapter 7 in Madeline and Senger Sirgay. *Emotional care of hospitalized children*. Philadelphia: J.B. Lippincott Co., 1972. 205.

McClelland, D.D. "The harlequin complex". in R.W. White ed. *The study of lives*. New York: Atherton Pr., 1963. 94-119.

McDonald, Marjorie. "A study of the reactions of nursery school children to the death of a child's mother". In v. 19 of *The psychoanalytic study of the child*. New York: International Universities Pr., Inc., 1964.

Mahler, Margaret S. "On sadness and grief in infancy and childhood - loss and restoration of the symbiotic love object". In v. 16 of Ruth S. Eissler et. al. *The psychoanalytic study of the child*. New York: International Universities Pr., Inc., 1960. 332-351.

Malinowski, Bronislaw. "Death and the reintegration of the group". In *Magic, Science and Religion*. New York: Doubleday & Co., Inc., 1954. 47-53.

Mandelbaum, David G. "Form, variation and meaning of a ceremony". In Robert F. Spencer ed. *Method and perspective in anthropology: papers in honor of Wilson D. Wallis*. Minneapolis: University of Minnesota Pr., 1954. 60-102.

Mann, Thomas. *The magic mountain*. New York: Alfred A. Knopf, Inc., 1958. 53.

Meiss, M. "The oedipal problem of a fatherless child". In v. 7 of *The psychoanalytic study of the child*. New York: International Universities Pr., 1952. 216-229.

Money-Kyrle, R.E. "An inconclusive contribution to the 'theory of the death instinct' ". In *New directions in psychoanalysis*. New York: Basic Books, 1955.

Morrissey, James R. "Death anxiety in children with a fatal illness". In Howard J. Parad ed. *Crisis intervention: selected readings*. New York: Family Service Association of America, 1965. 324-338.

Orwell, G. "How the poor die". In *Shooting an elephant*. New York: Harcourt, Brace & World, Inc., 1950. 25.

Parkes, C.M. "The psychosomatic effects of bereavement". In v. 2 of Oscar W. Hill ed. *Modern trends in psychosomatic medicine*. London: Butterworth, 1970.

Parsons, Talcott and Lidz, V. "Death in American society". In Edwin Shneidman ed. *Essays in self-destruction*. New York: Science House, 1967. 133-170.

Pattison, E. Mansell. "Help in the dying process". Chapter 34 in v. 1 of Silvano Arieti ed. *American handbook of psychiatry*. 2d ed. New York: Basic Books, Inc., Publishers, 1974. 685-702.

Paz, Octavio. "The day of the dead". In *Labyrinth of solitude: life and thought in Mexico*. New York: Grove Pr., 1961. 47-64.

Piaget, Jean. *The child's conception of physical causality*. London: Kegan Paul, 1930. 241-258.

Radcliffe-Brown, Alfred Reginald. "Taboo". In *Structure and function in primitive society*. London: Cohen and West, 1952. 133-152.

Reemtsma, K. "Ethical problems with artificial and transplanted organs: an approach by experiential ethics". In E.F. Torrey ed. *Ethical issues in medicine*. Boston: Little, Brown and Co., 1968. 249-263.

Rioch, D. et. al. "The psychophysiology of death". In A. Simon ed. *The physiology of emotions*. Springfield, Illinois: C.C. Thomas, 1961. 77-225.

Rivers, W.H.R. "The primitive conception of death". In H. Elliot Smith ed. *Psychology and ethnology*. New York: Harcourt Brace and Co., Inc., 1927. 36-50.

Rochlin, G. "Loss and restitution". In v. 8 of *The psychoanalytic study of the child*. New York: International Universities Pr., 1953. 288-309.

Rochlin, Gregory. "The dread of abandonment: a contribution to the etiology of the loss complex and to the depression". In v. 16 of *The psychoanalytic study of the child*. New York: International Universities Pr., Inc. 1961. 451-470.

Scharf, Adele E. "Regression and restitution in object-loss: clinical observations". In v. 16 of *The psychoanalytic study of the child*. New York: International Universities Pr., Inc., 1961. 471-480.

Schur, Max. "Discussion of Dr. John Bowlby's paper 'Grief and mourning in infancy and early childhood' ". In v. 5 of *The psychoanalytic study of the child*. New York: International Universities Pr., Inc., 1960. 63-84.

Shambaugh, B. "A study of loss reactions in a seven-year-old". In v. 16 of *The psychoanalytic study of the child*. New York: International Universities Pr., Inc., 1961. 510-552.

Shields, H. "The dead lover's return in modern English ballad tradition". In *Jahrbuch fur Volksleidforschung*. Berlin: Erich Schmidt Verlag, Jahrgang 16, 17, 1972. 98-114.

Siegel, Richard, Michael Strassfeld and Sharon Strassfeld. *The Jewish Catalog*. Philadelphia: The Jewish Publication Society of America, 1973. 172-181.

Slater, Philip E. "Prolegomena to a psychoanalytic theory of aging and death". In R. Kastenbaum ed. *New thoughts on old age*. New York: Springer, 1964. 38-55.

Sperry, Roger. "Mind, brain and humanist values". In John R. Platt ed. *New views of the nature of man*. Chicago: University of Chicago Pr., 1965.

Spitz, Rene A., assisted by Katherine M. Wolf. "Anaclitic depression - an inquiry into the genesis of psychiatric conditions in early childhood". In v. 2 of Ruth S. Eissler et. al. ed. *The psychoanalytic study of the child*. New York: International Universities Pr., Inc., 1946. 313-342.

Starzl, T.E. "Ethical problems in organ transplantation: a clinician's point of view". In J.R. Elkington ed. *The changing mores of biomedical research: a colloquium on ethical dilemmas for medical advances. Annals of Internal Medicine* 67 Suppl. 7:32-36, 1967.

Steinzor, Bernard. "Death and the construction of reality". In John G. Peatman and Eugene L. Hartley ed. *Festschrift for Gardner Murphy*. New York: Harper, 1960. 358-375.

Stone, Joseph L. and Joseph Church. *Childhood and adolescence*. New York: Random House, 1973. 135, 175, 289, 498.

Stonecypher, D.D., Jr. "Helping the survivors". In *Getting older and staying younger*. New York: W.W. Norton & Co., 1974. 171-178.

Stonecypher, D.D., Jr. "How the physician and the relative can help". In *Getting older and staying younger*. New York: W.W. Norton & Co., 1974. 163-170.

Stonecypher, D.D., Jr. "How we control our fear of death". In *Getting older and staying younger*. New York: W.W. Norton & Co., 1974. 147-153.

Stonecypher, D.D., Jr. "What do you say to a dying person". In *Getting older and staying younger*. New York: W.W. Norton & Co., 1974. 154-162.

Streib, Gordon and W.E. Thompson. "The older person in a family context". In *Handbook of social gerontology*. Chicago: University of Chicago Pr., 1960. 447-448.

Taylor, Gordon Rattray. *The biological time bomb*. New York: The World Publishing Co., 1974. 100-112.

"The terminally ill child". Chapters 16-27 in Gladys B. Lipkin. *Psychosocial aspects of maternal-child nursing*. St. Louis, Missouri: C.V. Mosby Co., 1974. 135-147.

"The terminally ill child". Chapter 29 in Gladys M. Scipien et. al. *Comprehensive pediatric nursing*. New York: McGraw-Hill Book Co., 1975. 423.

Thielicke, H. "The doctor as judge of who shall live and who shall die". In K. Vaux ed. *Who shall live? Medicine technology ethics*. Philadelphia: Fortress Pr., 1970. 146-194.

Thomlinson, Ralph. *Population dynamics: causes and consequences of world demographic change*. New York: Random House, Inc., 1965. 106-107.
Tylor, E.B. *Primitive culture*. London: Printed in the U.S.A., 1920. v. 1, Chapter 12.
Tzu, Hsun. "A discussion of rites". In Burton Watson, translator. *Hsun Tzu, basic writings*. New York: Columbia University Pr., 1963. 109-110.
Volkart, Edmund H. and Stanley T. Michael. "Bereavement and mental health". In A.H. Leighton, J.A. Clausen and R.N. Wilson ed. *Explorations in social psychology*. New York: Basic Books, 1957. 281-307.
Wallenchensky, David and Irving Wallace. "Afterlife and reincarnation". In *The people's almanac*. New York: Doubleday, 1975. 1334-1336.
Weisman, A.D. and R. Kastenbaum. "The psychological autopsy as a research procedure in gerontology". In D. Kent, R. Kastenbaum and S. Sherwood ed. *Research planning and action for the elderly*. New York: Behavioral Publications, 1972.
Weisman, Avery D. and Thomas P. Hacett. "Denial as a social act". In Sidney Levin and Ralph J. Kahana. *Psychodynamic studies on aging: creativity, reminiscing and dying*. New York: International Universities Pr., 1967.
Williams, Joyce Wolfgang and Marjorie Smith. *Middle childhood behavior and development*. New York: MacMillan Publishing Co., nc., 1974. 362-364.
Woehning, Marilee and Ida M. Martinson. "Family nursing during death and dying". Chapter 46 in Barbara W. Spradley. *Contemporary community nursing*. Boston: Little, Brown and Co., 1975. 405-413.

SPEECHES AND REPRINTED, MIMEOGRAPHED AND UNPUBLISHED PAPERS

Allen, Nancy H. and Michael L. Peck. *Suicide in young people*. West Point, Pennsylvania: Association of Suicidology in cooperation with Merck, Sharp and Dohme, Inc.
Anderson, Robert. "Playwright tells conference on death of 'playing God' in wife's last years". Rochester, New York, May 1, 1971. Reprint of AP report.

Cassem, N.H., Earl A. Grollman and Edgar N. Jackson. *Three religions view death*. The Dodge Institute seminars, 1974. reprint.
Die now, live later. Columbia, Ohio: Xerox Corporations, November, 1975.
"Dilemmas of euthanasia". New York Academy of Medicine, 4th Euthanasia Conference, December 4, 1971. Excerpts from papers and discussions.
Fast, Irene and Albert C. Cain. *Disturbances in parent-child relationships following bereavement*. University of Michigan, 1963. Unpublished paper.
Foster D. Snell, Inc., General Laboratories, Florham Park, New Jersey. *The antimicrobial activity of embalming chemicals and topical disinfectants on the microbial flora of human remains*. Boston: Dodge Chemical Co., March 19, 1973.
Frederick, Jerome. *Grief as a disease process: a physiological-endocrine model*. Bronx, New York: Dodge Chemical Co., the Research Laboratories. Printed exclusively for use by the Dodge Institute advanced mortuary studies seminars, Winter, 1976.
Hamovitch, Maurice B. *Parental reactions to the death of a child*. Duarte, California: City of Hope Medical Center, 1962. Mimeographed. 27 p.
Hinson, Maude R. *Final report on literature search on the infectious nature of dead bodies*. Embalming Chemical Manufacturer's Association, September 1, 1968.
Jackson, Edgar N. "Embalming and the perfect effigy". Unidentified reprint.
Lamers, William M., Jr. "Death, grief, mourning, the funeral and the child". Address given at the 84th Convention of the National Funeral Directors Association. Chicago, Illinois, November 1, 1965. Mimeographed. 14 p.
LaMore, George E., Jr. "This will be the death of all of us". Reprint of speech given at the Clergy/Funeral Directors Seminars sponsored by the Nebraska Funeral Directors Association.
MacPherson, Jennifer. "Euthanasia rights and realities". Luncheon speech. Fifth Euthanasia Conference, December 2, 1972. Excerpts from papers and discussions.
Oman, John. *Grief therapy*. Unidentified reprint.

Norman, Paul. *The mourning experience in family therapy.* Arlington, Massachusetts: Arlington Public Schools. Psychological Counseling Department, March, 1966. Unpublished paper.

Portz, Alexius T. *The psychological meaning of death: a review of the literature.* Third year paper. University of Michigan, Deparment of Psychology, June, 1963. Mimeographed.

Sandler, David. "The study of bereavement". In K.D. Kroupa and D. Sandler ed. *Community mental health: theory, practice and research.* Harvard University, 1962. Unpublished manuscript.

Silverman, Phyllis. *Proceedings of a workshop for widows and widowers,* sponsored by Widow-to-widow Program: Harvard Medical School, Boston, Massachusetts, June, 1971. (Mimeographed copies only).

Stevens, Roland. "Euthanasia: a doctor speaks". Reprint of a speech given at the Euthanasia Education Council, New York, February 4, 1971.

Workshop on the terminally ill patient and helping persons. "The dying person's bill of rights". Lansing, Michigan: Southwestern Michigan Inservice Education Council reprint.

GOVERNMENT DOCUMENTS

Beckwith, J. Bruce. *Sudden infant death syndrome.* 1975. (DHEW publication (HSA) 75-5137; Office of Maternal and Child Health).

Bibliography on suicide and suicide prevention, 1897-1957, 1958-1967. Chevy Chase, Maryland: National Institote of Mental Health, 1969.

Leviton, D. *Death education and change in students' attitudes; final report.* Public Health Service Grant MH 21974-01. Washington, D.C.: Department of Health, Education and Welfare, 1973.

"Quiet Cries", For free single copy write: "Quiet Cries", Public Inquiries, National Institute of Mental Health, 5600 Fishers Lane, Rockville, MD 20852, Additional copies at $.25 each, write Superintendent of Documents, U.S. Government Printing Office, Washington, D.C. (Play)

Resnik, H.L.P. and Berkley C. Hathorne ed. *Suicide prevention in the 70's.* Rockville, Maryland: U.S. National Institute of Mental

Health. Center for Studies of Suicide Prevention. (DHEW Publication No. (HSM) 72-9054). 1973.

U.S. Congress. Senate. Special Committee on Aging. Subcommittee on Frauds and Misrepresentation Affecting the Elderly. *Health frauds and quackery, hearings*. 88th Congress, 2d Session.

U.S. Defense Department. Army Medical Service. *Symposium on preventive and social psychiatry* April 15-17, 1957. Walter Reed Army Institute of Research, Washington, D.C., 1958. Sponsored jointly by Walter Reed Army Institute, Walter Reed Army Medical Center and the National Research Council.

U.S. Department of Health, Education and Welfare. *The facts of life and death*. Washington, D.C.: Public Health Service Publication No. 600, Revised edition, 1965.

U.S. Department of Health Education and Welfare. *Hospitalization during the last year of life: United States, 1961*. Washington, D.C.: Public Health Service Publication No. 1000, series 22, no. 1, 1965.

U.S. Department of Health, Education and Welfare. National Institute of Health. *Early diagnosis of human genetic effects, scientific and ethical consideration, symposium* sponsored by John E. Fogarty International Center for Advanced Study in Health Sciences, National Institutes of Health, Bethesda, Maryland, May 18-19, 1970. Maureen Harris ed. 1971. (HEW publication (NIH 72-25).

U.S. Department of Health, Education and Welfare. National Institute of Health. *Sudden infant death syndrome; selected* annotated bibliography, 1960-1971. Prepared by Scientific Publications Section, Office of Public Information. 1972. (DHEW publication; (NIH) 72-237.)

U.S. National Center for Health Statistics. *Funeral directors' handbook on death and fetal death registration*. Washington, D.C.: U.S. Government Printing Office, 1967.

U.S. Senate Committee on the Judiciary. Subcommittee on Antitrust and Monopoly. *Antitrust aspects of the funeral industry* Hearings. Washington, D.C.: USGPO, 1964.

Vernick, Joel J. *Selected bibliography on death and dying*. Washington, D.C.: U.S. National Institutes of Health, 1969.

Wecht, Cyril H. *The medico-legal autopsy laws of the fifty states, the District of Columbia, American Samoan, the Canal Zone,*

Guam, Puerto Rico, and the Virgin Islands. Washington, D.C.: Armed Forces Institute of Pathology, 1971.

World Health Organization. *Manual of the International Statistical Classification of diseases, injuries and causes of death.* Based on the Recommendations of the 8th Revision Conference, 1965 and adapted by the 19th World Health Assembly, Geneva, 1967. 2 vols.

THESES AND DISSERTATIONS

Abrahamsson, Hans. *The origin of death: studies in African mythology.* Unpublished thesis, Upsala College, 1951.

Adlerstein, Arthur M. *The relationship between religious belief and death affect.* Doctoral dissertation, Princeton University, 1958. 155 p. *Dissertation Abstracts,* 19/11: 3016, 1959.

Baird, Carol Friedell. *Death fantasy in male and female college students* Doctoral dissertation, Boston University Graduate School, 1972. 159 p. *Dissertation Abstracts,* 33/04B: 1778, 1972.

Bascue, Loy Orn. *A study of the relationship of time orientation and time attitudes to death anxiety in elderly people.* Doctoral dissertation, University of Maryland, 1972. 108 p. *Dissertation Abstracts,* 34/02B: 866, 1973.

Behren, R. et. al. *A descriptive study of elementary school children who have sustained a major loss.* Unpublished master's thesis. Simmons College of Social Work, June, 1964.

Blake, Robert Richmond. *Attitudes toward death as a function of developmental stages.* Doctoral dissertation, Northwestern University, 1969. 113 p. *Dissertation Abstracts,* 30/07B: 388, 1970.

Blum, Alan Howard. *Children's conceptions of death and an after-life.* Doctoral dissertation, State University of New York at Buffalo, 1975. *Dissertation Abstracts,* 36/10B: 5248, 1976.

Brown, David Jeffrey. *The fear of death and the western-protestant ethic personality identity.* Doctoral dissertation, Ohio State University, 1971. 154 p. *Dissertation Abstracts,* 32/12B: 7302, 1972.

Buch, Lee Charles. *Death scales: a factor study.* Doctoral dissertation, Kent State University, 1975. 116 p. *Dissertation Abstracts,* 36/12B:6371, 1976.

Burrows, Arlene Blaier. *Fear of death and attitudes toward death as a function of religion.* Doctoral dissertation, State University of New York at Buffalo, 1971. 136 p. *Dissertation Abstracts,* 32/03B: 3630, 1971.

Carson, William J. *Modes of coping with death concern.* Doctoral dissertation, University of Missouri at Columbia, 1973. 170 p. *Dissertation Abstracts,* 35/02A: 815, 1974.

Chellan, Grace. *The disengagement theory: an awareness of death and self-engagement.* Doctoral dissertation, Western Reserve University, 1964. 155 p. *Dissertation Abstracts,* 25/11: 6806, 1965.

Dickinson, Arlene K. *Nurses' perception of their care of patients dying with cancer.* Doctoral dissertation, Columbia University, 1966. 252 p. *Dissertation Abstracts,* 27/04B: 402, 1966.

Dobihal, Edward Frank, Jr. *Bereavement and the church's ministry (an exploratory study involving spouses of deceased church members.)* Doctoral dissertation, Drew University, 1965. 275 p. *Dissertation Abstracts,* 26/05: 2888, 1965.

Eichmann, Andrew Eugene. *A comparison of groups differing on religious variables on several attitudes toward death.* Doctoral dissertation, Fordham University, 1974. 110 p. *Dissertation Abstracts,* 35/03B: 1401, 1974.

Emerson, Joan. *Social functions of humor in a hospital.* Doctoral dissertation, University of California-Berkeley, 1963. 396 p. *Dissertation Abstracts,* 24/12: 5586, 1964.

Farley, Gail Ann. *An investigation of death anxiety and the sense of competence.* Doctoral dissertation, Duke University, 1970. 173 p. *Dissertation Abstracts,* 31/12B: 7595, 1971.

Fisher, Bradley. *Self-exploration experience in death encounter.* Doctoral dissertation, University of Florida, 1968. 106 p. *Dissertation Abstracts,* 30/05A: 1819, 1969.

Fleming, Stephen J. *Nurses' death anxiety and clinical geriatric training.* Doctoral dissertation, York University (Canada), 1974. *Dissertation Abstracts,* 36/10B: 5254, 1976.

Fortier, Millie Kelley. *Dreams and preparation for death.* Doctoral dissertation, California School of Professional Psychology, 1972. 190 p. *Dissertation Abstracts,* 33/07: 3300, 1973.

Fulcomer, David M. *The adjustive behavior of some recently bereaved spouses.* Doctoral dissertation, Northwestern University, 1942. 134 p.

Giesey, Ralph E. *The royal funeral ceremony in renaissance France*. Doctoral dissertation, University of California at Berkeley, 1954. 230 p.

Greenberger, Ellen. *Fantasies of women confronting death: a study of critically ill patients*. Doctoral dissertation, Radcliffe College, 1961. 179 p.

Gullo, Stephen Viton. *A study of selected psychological, psychosomatic and somatic reactions in women anticipating the death of a husband*. Doctoral dissertation, Columbia University, 1974. 169 p. *Dissertation Abstracts*, 35/10B: 5113, 1975.

Habenstein, Robert W. *The American funeral director; a study in the sociology of work*. Doctoral dissertation, University of Chicago, 1955. 930 p.

Handal, Paul John. *Orientation as a function of repression-sensitization of death anxiety*. Doctoral dissertation, St. Louis University, 1970. 98 p. *Dissertation Abstracts*, 31/05B: 2986, 1970.

Hansen, Yvonne F. *Development of the concept of death--cognitive aspects*. Doctoral dissertation, California School of Professional Psychology, 1973. 152 p. *Dissertation Abstracts*, 34/02B: 853, 1973.

Hardt, Dale Vincent. *Development of an investigatory instrument to measure attitudes toward death*. Doctoral dissertation, Southern Illinois University, 1974. 127 p. *Dissertation Abstracts*, 36/02B: 646, 1975.

Hineman, Joseph H. *Counseling with the terminally ill: a clinical study*. Doctoral dissertation, University of Utah, 1971. 132 p. *Dissertation Abstracts*, 32/06A: 3091, 1971.

Hoblit, Pamela R. *An investigation of changes in anxiety level following consideration of death in four groups*. Doctoral dissertation, Louisiana State University and Agricultural and Mechanical College, 1971. 59 p. *Dissertation Abstracts*, 33/05B: 2346, 1972.

Kasmarik, Patricia E. *Attitude score changes toward death and dying in nursing students*. Doctoral dissertation, Columbia University, 1974. 94 p. *Dissertation Abstracts*, 35/04B: 1767, 1974.

Klopfer, W.G. *Attitudes toward death in the aged*. Master's thesis, City College, New York, 1947.

Koocher, Gerald P. *Childhood, death and cognitive development*. Doctoral dissertation, University of Missouri, 1972. 90 p. *Dissertation Abstracts*, 33/09B: 4512, 1973.

Langer, Lawrence. *The fear of death; an exploratory study*. Doctoral dissertation, Michigan State University, 1975. 179 p. *Dissertation Abstracts*, 36/09B: 4694, 1976.

Lowry, Richard J. *Male-female differences in attitudes toward death*. Doctoral dissertation, Brandeis University, 1965. *Dissertation Abstracts*, 27/05B: 1607, 1966.

Lucas, Richard A. *A comparative study of measures of general anxiety and death anxiety among three medical groups including patient and wife*. Doctoral dissertation, University of North Carolina at Chapel Hill, 1972. 205 p. *Dissertation Abstracts*, 33/03B: 1290, 1972.

McCarthy, James Brian. *Death anxiety, intrinsicness of religion and purpose in life among Nuns and Roman Catholic female undergraduates*. Doctoral dissertation, St. John's University, 1973. 120 p. *Dissertation Abstracts*, 35/11B: 5646, 1975.

Malcolm, Thomas Jonathan. *The effects of ease on denial on perceiving and adapting to ideas about personal death*. Doctoral dissertation, Fuller Theological Seminary Graduate School of Psychology, 1972. 194 p. *Dissertation Abstracts*, 33/07B: 3351, 1973.

Mednick, Robert Anthony. *Content and frequency of sexual fantasy as a function of the frequency and content of death fantasy and death anxiety*. Doctoral dissertation, International University, 1975. 325 p. *Dissertation Abstracts*, 36/04B: 1924, 1975.

Melear, John. *Children's conception of death*. Doctoral dissertation, University of Northern Colorado, 1972. 164 p. *Dissertation Abstracts*, 33/02B: 919, 1972.

Miller, Jill Mener. *The effects of aggressive stimulation upon young adults who have experienced the death of a parent during childhood*. Doctoral dissertation, New York University, 1972. 116 p. *Dissertation Abstracts*, 35/02B: 1055, 1974.

Moriarity, James J.P. *Death anxiety in hysteric and obsessive personalities*. Doctoral dissertation, University of Detroit, 1974. 141 p. *Dissertation Abstracts*, 36/08B: 4169, 1976.

Moses, Michael. *Considering death and dying: affective correlates*. Doctoral dissertation, State University of New York at Buffalo, 1973. 147 p. *Dissertation Abstracts*, 34/02B: 877, 1973.

Mullaly, Robert William. *Death-dying fears and psychopathology in psychiatric patients.* Doctoral dissertation, University of Tennessee, 1975. 150 p. *Dissertation Abstracts,* 36/03B: 1448, 1975.

Myler, Beatrice B. *Depression and death in the aged.* Doctoral dissertation, Boston University, 1967. 149 p. *Dissertation Abstracts,* 28/15B: 2146, 1967.

Nightingale, John Anthony. *The relationship of Jungian type to death concern and time perspective.* Doctoral dissertation, University of South Carolina, 1972. 77 p. *Dissertation Abstracts,* 33/08B: 3956, 1973.

Odell, Jeanne Lucille. *The psychodynamics observed in a stratified-cultural study of death: a phenomenological approach.* Doctoral dissertation, U.S. International University, 1975. 223 p. *Dissertation Abstracts,* 35/11B: 5623, 1975.

Parkes, C.M. *Morbid grief reactions: a review of the literature.* Doctoral dissertation, University of London, 1959.

Parkin, James Michael. *Assignment of responsibility for deaths perceived as unintentioned, subintentioned or intentioned.* Doctoral dissertation, Purdue University, 1971. 44 p. *Dissertation Abstracts,* 32/98B: 4867, 1972.

Peck, Rosalind *The development of the concept of death in selected male children: an experimental investigation of the development of the concept of death in selected children from the point of no concept to the point where a fully developed concept is attained with an investigation of some factors which may affect the course of concept development.* Doctoral dissertation, New York University, 1966. 136 p. *Dissertation Abstracts,* 27/04B: 1294, 1966.

Pepitone-Rockwell, Frances Marie. *Death anxiety of psychologists, psychiatrists, funeral directors, and suicidologists.* Doctoral dissertation, California School of Professional Psychology, 1974. 129 p. *Dissertation Abstracts,* 35/06B: 3030, 1974.

Pratt, Earle Wilson, Jr. *A death education laboratory as a medium for influencing feelings toward death.* Doctoral dissertation, U.S. International University, 1974. 159 p. *Dissertation Abstracts,* 34/08B: 4026, 1974.

Rawlins, Grant Clement. *An exploratory study of some psychological implications of the death penalty as measured on the MMPI of convicted murders.* Doctoral dissertation, California School of Professional Psychology, 1976. 68 p. *Dissertation Abstracts,* 36/11B: 5813, 1976.

Redick, Robert J. *Behavorial group counseling and death anxiety in student nurses.* Thesis, University of Pittsburgh, 1974.

Rees, W.D. *The hallucinatory and paranormal reactions of bereavement.* MD thesis, 1970.

Romero, Carol E. *The treatment of death in contemporary children's literature.* Master's thesis, Long Island University, 1974. Also available as ERIC Document ED 101 664 (Microfiche).

Sell, Irene Louise. *Guide to materials on death and dying for teachers of nursing.* Doctoral dissertation, Colorado University, 1975. 227 p. *Dissertation Abstracts,* 36/03B: 1151, 1975.

Selvey, Carol Light. *Concern about death in relation to sex, dependency, guilt about hostility and feelings of powerlessness.* Doctoral dissertation, Columbia University, 31/09B: 5641, 1971.

Smith, Alexander Hamilton, Jr. *A multivariate study of factor analyzed predictors of death anxiety in college students.* Doctoral dissertation, University of Cincinnati, 1975. 112 p. *Dissertation Abstracts,* 36/07B: 3585, 1976.

Smith, Helen C. *Care of the dying patient: a comparison of instructional plans.* Doctoral dissertation, Indiana University, 1965. 106 p. *Dissertation Abstracts,* 27/02B: 526, 1966.

Smith, Walter John. *The desolation of Dido: patterns of depression and death anxiety in the adjustment and adaptation behaviors of a sample of variably-aged widows.* Doctoral dissertation, Boston University Graduate School, 1975. 260 p. *Dissertation Abstracts,* 36/04B: 1933, 1975.

Spinetta, John Joseph. *Death anxiety in leukemic children.* Doctoral dissertation, University of Southern California, 1972. 195 p. *Dissertation Abstracts,* 33/04B: 1807, 1972.

Steiner, Gloria L. *Children's concepts of life and death: a developmental study.* Doctoral dissertation, Columbia University, 1965. 140 p. *Dissertation Abstracts,* 26/02: 1164, 1965.

Szabo, Karen. *Death education: rationale and methodology for age-graded courses.* Unpublished Master's thesis, College of Human Development, Pennsylvania State University, 1973.

Templer, Donald Irwin. *The construction and validation of a death anxiety scale*. Doctoral dissertation, University of Kentucky, 1967. 77 p. *Dissertation Abstracts*, 30/05B: 2410, 1969.

Votau, Thomas Edward. *Death anxiety in black and white elderly subjects in institutionalized and non-institutionalized settings*. Doctoral dissertation, Auburn University, 1974. 88 p. *Dissertation Abstracts*, 35/03B: 1420, 1974.

Waechter, Eugenia H. *Death anxiety in children with fatal illness*. Doctoral dissertation, Stanford University, 1968. 192 p. *Dissertation Abstracts*, 29/07B: 2505, 1959.

Walworth, Joy Harold. *Conceptions of death and dying in personal poetry*. Doctoral dissertation, California School of Professional Psychology, 1972. 114 p. *Dissertation Abstracts*, 33/07B: 3327, 1973.

Wells, James Ogdin II. *An experimental study of the assignment of responsibility for unintentioned, subintentioned and intentioned death*. Doctoral dissertation, George Washington University, 1970. 126 p. *Dissertation Abstracts*, 31/04B: 2294, 1970.

Wesch, Jerry E. *Self-actualization and the fear of death*. Doctoral dissertation, University of Tennessee, 1970. 85 p. *Dissertation Abstracts*, 31/10B: 6270, 1971.

Zeitlin, Steven J. *The effect of recent father death on adolescent identity formation*. Doctoral dissertation, Harvard University, 1975. 312 p. *Dissertation Abstracts*, 36/09B: 4716, 1976.

Zhianai-Rezai, Z. *Doctors and death*. Doctoral dissertation, University of Oregon, 1968. 177 p. *Dissertation Abstracts*, 30/02B: 839, 1969.

PAMPHLETS

Alerting bereaved families: a special bulletin. Indianapolis: Better Business Bureau, Inc., 1961.

American Hospital Association. *Statement on a patient's bill of rights*. 1972. (Reprinted in John A. Behnke and Sissela Bok ed. *The dilemmas of euthanasia*. Garden City, New York: Doubleday, 1975. Appendix 2, 157-159).

Answers to questions about funeral costs. Milwaukee, Wisconsin: National Funeral Directors Association, September, 1975.

Appointed once to die. Milwaukee, Wisconsin: National Funeral Directors Association.

Bump, Ronald I. *What is grief?* Lincoln, Nebraska: The Grief Center.

Caroline, Nancy L. *Do doctors know the real enemy?* New York: The Euthanasia Educational Council.

The Catholic burial rite. Milwaukee, Wisconsin: National Funeral Directors Association.

The challenge of transplantation. Milwaukee, Wisconsin: National Funeral Directors Association.

Clothier, Florence. *Euthanasia - the physician's dilemma*. New York, The Euthanasia Educational Council, November 19, 1972.

Code of professional practices for funeral directors. Milwaukee, Wisconsin: National Funeral Directors Association.

The condolence or sympathy visit. Milwaukee, Wisconsin: National Funeral Directors Association.

Considerations concerning cremation. Milwaukee, Wisconsin: National Funeral Directors Association, 1974.

"Dealing With the Crisis of Suicide", 20 pages - 1972 - No. 406A, Public Affairs Pamphlets, 381 Park Avenue South, New York, NY 10016, $.35/copy.

"Death Education as a Learning Experience" by Loren Bensley, Jr., Special Current Issues No. 3, SCIPS, ERIC Clearinghouse on Teacher Education, Suite 616, One Dupont Circle, Washington, D.C. 20036.

Doyle, Nancy. *The dying person and the family*. New York: Public Affairs Pamphlets.

"The Dying Person and the Family", Public Affairs Commission, 381 Park Avenue South, NY 10016, $.35/copy.

An essay on the problems related to the prolongation of life by technological methods. United Presbyterian Church, 186th General Assembly, 1974. Available from the Unit on Church and Society, 475 Riverside Dr., Room 1244K, New York, N.Y. 10027.

Euthanasia Educational Council. *A living will*. Euthanasia Educational Council, 250 W. 57th St., New York, N.Y. (Reprinted in John A. Behnke and Sissela Bok ed. *The dilemmas of euthanasia*. Garden City, New York: Doubleday, 1975. Appendix 1, 153-156).

Facts every family should know. Forest Park, Illinois: Wilbert, Inc., 1972.

Facts every family should know about funerals and interments. New York: Association of Better Business Bureaus, Inc., 1961.

Frederick, Calvin J. and L. Lague. *Dealing with crisis of suicide*. New York: Public Affairs Pamphlets.

The funeral: facing death as an experience of life - an historical review; a contemporary overview; change in the future. Milwaukee, Wisconsin: National Funeral Directors Association.

The funeral from ancient Egypt to present day America. An illustrated historical documentary. Milwaukee, Wisconsin: National Funeral Directors Association.

The Grief Center. Lincoln, Nebraska: The Grief Center.

"Grief and Mourning", Department of Mental Health, Office of Preventive Programs, P.O. Box 178, Frankfort, KY 40601. $.25/copy.

How to meet a family crisis. Milwaukee Wisconsin: National Funeral Directors Association.

"How to Prevent Suicide", 28 pages, 1967-Schneidman and Mandlekorn, Public Affairs Pamphlets, 381 Park Avenue South, New York, NY 10016, $.35/copy.

How would you tell your son that his Grandpa died. Milwaukee, Wisconsin; National Funeral Directors Association.

Income and outgo. Hartford, Connecticut: LIAMA.

Irion, Paul E. *The funeral - an experience of value*. Milwaukee, Wisconsin: National Funeral Directors Association.

Irion, Paul E. *Humanist funeral service*. Milwaukee, Wisconsin: National Funeral Directors Association.

The law and the right to grieve. Milwaukee, Wisconsin: National Funeral Directors Association.

Like a ship's rudder. Hastings, Nebraska: Nebraska Funeral Directors.

Memorials of a nation: America remembers her people, 1776-1976. Peoria, Illinois: Dimensional Services Co., 1975.

Miller, D.F. *Program for widows*. Liguari, Missouri: Redemptarist Fathers, Liguarian Pamphlets, 1961.

Mundhenke, Clarke A. *When children ask about death*. Lincoln, Nebraska: Lincoln General Hospital, School of Nursing Library.

National Funeral Directors Association. *Funeral service as a profession*. Milwaukee, Wisconsin: National Funeral Directors Association, 1963.

The organ donor program. Lincoln, Nebraska: Kidney Foundation of Nebraska.

Osborne, Ernest G. *When you lose a loved one*. New York: Public Affairs Committee, 1958. (Public Affairs Pamphlet No. 269).
Personal papers, records. Hartford, Connecticut: LIAMA.
The pre-arranging and pre-financing of funerals. Milwaukee, Wisconsin: National Funeral Directors Association.
The right to die with dignity. New York: Euthanasia Educational Council, April, 1974.
Sheldon, Roderick. *Bible light on modern funeral service customs*. Milwaukee, Wisconsin: National Funeral Directors Association.
The significance of the Christian funeral. Milwaukee, Wisconsin: National Funeral Directors Association.
Slater, Robert C. ed. *Funeral service, meeting needs . . . serving people*. Milwaukee, Wisconsin: National Funeral Directors Association, 1974.
Some thoughts to consider when arranging a funeral. Milwaukee, Wisconsin: National Funeral Directors Association.
Someone you love has died; some thoughts and suggestions about funerals. Milwaukee, Wisconsin: National Funeral Directors Association.
Taylor, Frank. *Suicide; the will to die*. U.S.A.: National Association of Blue Shield Plans, 1973.
Too personal to be private. Milwaukee, Wisconsin: National Funeral Directors Association.
Understanding your life insurance. New York: The Institute of Life Insurance.
What about funeral costs. Milwaukee, Wisconsin: National Funeral Directors Association.
What do you really know about funeral costs. Milwaukee, Wisconsin: National Funeral Directors Association.
What does she do now? Hartford, Connecticut: LIAMA.
What every doctor should know about the religious needs of his patient. Chicago: Illinois State Medical Society. Committee on Medicine and Religion.
When a death occurs . . . needs . . . concerns . . . decisions. Milwaukee, Wisconsin: Natiokal Funeral Directors Association.
"When You Lose a Loved One" (printed matter), Public Affairs Commission, 381 Park Avenue South, New York, NY 10016, $.35/copy.
A wife looks at life insurance. New York: The Institute of Life Insurance.

With the body present. Milwaukee, Wisconsin: National Funeral Directors Association.

Wolf, Anna. *Your child's emotional health*. Public Affairs Pamphlet No. 264, 1958.

Your life insurance and how it works. New York: The Institute of Life Insurance.

SURVEYS AND PAPERS PRESENTED AT MEETINGS

Anderson, Herbert. *Learning and Teaching About Death and Dying*. Princeton Theological Seminary, New Jersey, 1972. 18p. ED 075 728 MF & HC.

Apseloff, Marilyn. *Death in current children's fiction: sociology of literature*. Paper presented at the Forum on the Criticism of Children's Literature of the Midwest Modern Language Association, St. Louis, Missouri, 1974. (Eric Document ED 101 371 available on microfiche).

Banta, Thomas J. *The Kennedy assassination: early thoughts and emotions*. Paper presented to the meeting of the Midwest Psychological Association, St. Louis, 1964.

Bennett, Roger V. *Death and the curriculum*. Paper presented at a meeting of the American Educational Research Association, Chicago, 1974. (Eric Document ED 093 782, available on microfiche).

Berg, David W. and George G. Daugherty. *Death education: a survey and study of colleges and universities*. Milwaukee, Wisconsin: National Funeral Directors Association.

Council for Christian Social Action of the United Church of Christ. *The right to die*. February 17, 1973.

Curphey, Theodore J. *The role of the forensic pathologist in the multidisciplinary approach to death*. Paper presented to the annual meeting of the American Psychological Association, Los Angeles, 1964.

Death and Dying: Attitudes of Patient and Doctor Symposium, Group for the Advancement of Psychiatry, New York, New York 10016, $2/copy.

Diggory, James C. *Death and self-esteem*. Paper presented to the meeting of the American Psychological Association, St. Louis, 1962.

Euthanasia rights and realities. New York Academy of Medicine, 5th Uthanasia Conference, December 2, 1972. Excerpts from papers and discussions.

Findings of the professional census. Milwaukee, Wisconsin: National Funeral Directors Association, 1969.

Fleming, Joan et. al. *The influence of parent loss in childhood on personality development and ego-structure.* Paper read at the meeting of the American Psychoanalytic Association, San Francisco, 1958.

Jeffers, Frances C. and Adriaan Verwoerdt. *Factors associated with frequency of death thoughts in elderly community volunteers.* Paper presented to the 7th International Congress of Gerontology, Vienna, Austria, July, 1966.

Kastenbaum, Robert. *The interpersonal context of death in a geriatric institution.* Paper presented at the 17th annual scientific meeting of the Gerontological Society, Minneapolis, October, 1964.

Koocher, Gerald P. *Talking about death with 'normal' children (research strategies issues).* Boston: The Children's Hospital Medical Center, Developmental Evaluation Clinic, 1973. Available as Eric Document ED 082 853 on microfiche.

Kubler-Ross, Elisabeth. "Coping patterns of patients who know their diagnosis". *Catastrophic illness in the 70's: critical issues and complex decisions: proceedings.* 4th National Symposium of Cancer Care, Inc. National Cancer Foundation, New York, October 15-16, 1970.

Liberman, Morton A. *Vulnerability to stress and the processes of dying.* Paper presented at the 7th International Congress of Gerontology, Vienna, Austria, July, 1966.

McLaughlin, N. and Robert Kastenbaum. *Engrossment in personal past, future and death.* Paper presented at the annual meeting of the American Psychological Association, September 2, 1966.

Nuckols, Robert C. "Widow's study". v. 1, Life Insurance Agency Management Association Report, No. 1970-8-730, v. 1, *The on-set of widowhood.* JSAS microfiche MS No. 296. No. 1970-8-730, v. 1, Technical Supplement. JSAS microfiche No. 297, No. 1971-4-730, v. 2. *Adjustment to widowhood, the first two years.* JSAS microfiche MS No. 298.

Organ and tissue transplantation and body donation. Milwaukee, Wisconsin: National Funeral Directors Association.

Payne, Edmund C., Jr. *The dying patient.* Paper presented at the Boston Society for Gerontologic Psychiatry, 1964.

Philibert, M. *Death, the 'unspoken variable' in gerontology and aging.* Paper presented to the 27th meeting of the Gerontological Society, 1974.

Rappaport, Alfred. *An analysis of funeral service pricing and quotation methods.* Milwaukee, Wisconsin: National Funeral Directors Association.

The right to die with dignity. The Euthanasia Educational Council, First Euthanasia Conference, November 23, 1968.

Robin, E.P. *Death and dying in children's readers.* Paper presented to the 27th meeting of the Gerontological Society, 1974.

Rosow, Irving and Grace Chellam. *An awareness of death-scale.* Paper presented at the 7th International Congress of Gerontology, Vienna, Austria, July, 1966.

Seigman, Aron W. *Background and personality factors associated with feelings and attitudes about death.* Paper presented at the meeting of the Society for Scientific Study of Religion, Cambridge, Massachusetts, 1961.

Scher, Jordan. *On death: the final construction.* Paper presented at the annual meeting of the American Psychological Association, Los Angeles, 1964.

Sheatsley, Paul B. and Norman M. Bradburn. *Assassination! How the American public responded.* University of Chicago. National Opinion Research Center. Paper read at the annual meeting of the American Psychological Association, Los Angeles, September, 1964.

Stephenson, Carol Ann. *Coping with death.* Paper presented at the 49th annual meeting of the Southwestern Sociological Association, 1974.

Teahan, John E. and S. Golin. *Reactions to the President's assassination as a function of sex ideology, perceived parental attitudes, and symbolic significance.* Paper presented to the meeting of the Midwest Psychological Association, St. Louis, 1964.

Death and attitudes toward death. Proceedings of Symposium on death and attitudes toward death, Minneapolis: Bell Museum of Pathology, 1972.

Vernon, Glenn M. *Attitudes toward death*. Paper presented at the annual meeting of the Society for the Scientific Study of Religion, New York City, October 30, 1965.

Vernon, Glenn M. *Changing interpretations of death*. Paper presented at the 34th annual meeting of the Southern Sociological Society, 1971.

Wheeler, Allan L. *The dying person: a deviant in the medical subculture*. Paper presented at the 37th annual meeting, Southern Sociological Society, 1974.

Woolf, Kurt. "Fear of death must be overcome in psychotherapy of the aged". Report delivered at the meeting of the Gerontological Society, 1966. Available in *Frontiers of Hospital Psychiatry*.

Wrightsman, Lawrence S. and G. C. Noble. *Reactions to the President's assassination and changes in philosophies of human nature*. Paper presented to the meeting of the Midwest Psychological Association, St. Louis, 1964.